How to Make Nothing but
MONEY

Discovering Your Hidden Opportunities for Wealth

Dave Del Dotto

Simon and Schuster

New York London Toronto Sydney Tokyo Singapore

Simon and Schuster
Simon & Schuster Building
Rockefeller Center
1230 Avenue of the Americas
New York, New York 10020

Designed by Irving Perkins Associates
Manufactured in the United States of America

Library of Congress Cataloging in Publication data

Del Dotto, Dave.
How to make nothing but money.

1. Real estate investment. I. Title.
HD1382.5.D46   1990   332.63'24   89-21884

ISBN 0-671-63858-0

This publication is designed to provide accurate and authoritative information in regard to the subject matter covered. It is sold with the understanding
that the author and publisher are not engaged in rendering legal or accounting service. If legal advice or other expert assistance is required, the services
of a competent professional person should be sought.

Adapted from a Declaration of
Principles jointly adopted by a
committee of the American Bar
Association and the Committee of
Publishers and Associations

BOMC offers recordings and compact discs, cassettes
and records. For information and catalog write to
BOMR, Camp Hill, PA 17012.

To all my employees in Del Dotto Enterprises, with thanks for doing their jobs so well that I can spend most of my time in Hawaii.

Table of Contents

Preface

Anyone who tells you there are secrets to becoming successful and wealthy is wrong. I know, because I spent years looking for those secrets. My search taught me how to make millions of dollars and introduced me to a richer life than I had ever imagined for myself; but it also showed me that there are no secrets to success. There are simply hidden opportunities, and many of them lie right before our eyes, once we learn how to recognize them.

Of course, it's understandable that I once thought wealthy people shared some mysterious knowledge that they kept from the rest of the world. Those of us who lived in the working-class neighborhood where I grew up never came in contact with the kinds of people who had all the money they could ever need. We knew, in a vague sort of way, that such people existed. But somehow we didn't believe they could be ordinary people like ourselves.

At a young age I promised myself I'd learn the mysterious formulas others had used to accumulate riches and then apply them to make myself a fortune. Not only that, but I determined to overcome the barriers of privilege set up by the very rich and to share this carefully guarded knowledge with anyone else who wanted it. Once I learned how to become rich, I planned to help every man and woman who started out at the bottom of the economic heap the way I did—without inherited wealth, without fancy private schooling, without special privilege—to have a chance to become as prosperous as he or she desired to be.

In pursuit of those secrets I read books, talked to successful people, attended seminars, listened to tapes, and studied every method anyone recommended as a route to wealth. Along the way I learned a great many useful things, as well as many more that were worse than useless.

The main fact I uncovered, though, was both encouraging and disappointing. Disappointing, because I learned there really are no magic words that will open the door to making as much money as you want without effort; encouraging, because anyone who truly wants to actually can become wealthy, often in a surprisingly short time. Techniques available to anyone who takes the trouble to search them out can be used to generate money in almost any amount.

You simply have to be willing to make the effort to learn to apply these techniques. You must spend some time planning and studying, and discipline yourself to change your habits somewhat. Instead of spending every evening and weekend watching television or visiting with friends, you have to be willing to defer some of those pleasures and devote more of your leisure hours to learning what to do and then actually doing it. The rewards far outweigh the sacrifices. Accomplishment will increase your confidence and enthusiasm for what you're doing, just as the added financial gain will raise your standard of living.

When I'd learned enough of these techniques, I found they became a new habit, a way of seeing the world that I'd never realized before. Hidden opportunities started popping up in places I'd never dreamed of looking. To a young man who once had trouble paying average bills, it was like gaining the Midas touch, as though I could simply walk through life making nothing but money everywhere I turned.

I suddenly realized that the seemingly insurmountable barriers, the apparently solid walls between the haves and the have-nots, were really made of tissue paper for anyone who had the energy, the determination, and the knowledge. I put some of the things I'd learned into a set of instructional materials and started teaching seminars. Soon students of mine were changing their lives and

10

making more money in less time, and with less effort, than they had ever dreamed possible. More and more invitations to speak were followed by requests for more information.

In six years my program grew into the Cash Flow System course, and it's been an amazing journey in a very short time. My course and I have been featured in leading national magazines such as *Money, Newsweek,* and *Time.* Television and radio programs requested interviews, and I started my own television program. Now I've been asked to present as much of my Cash Flow System as possible in this book.

Choosing what to include here hasn't been easy. There are so many ideas I want to share with you in a limited space, and it's difficult to know which ones will help the most people in such a wide and diverse public. Finally I decided to give you the basic outlines of several of the most valuable and popular parts of my course. You can choose the sections that hold the most value and offer the best opportunities for your own situation and pursue them as far as your interest and energy take you.

In addition, I've tucked in many short ideas and inspirational case histories as separate sections called "Moneymakers." Where I've used people's actual case histories I've usually changed their names to protect their privacy, but each is a real-life example of a way someone can increase positive cash flow and come closer to financial independence.

I hope you'll accept these ideas in the same spirit I offer them to you. They are there for you to take and use. It's my sincere wish that you'll find at least one you can put into practice right away to help you, too, make nothing but money.

Wealth, health, and happiness to you,
Dave Del Dotto

PART I

A Foot in the Door to Financial Independence

CHAPTER 1

Your Strategy for Acquiring Wealth

There are only three ways the average, honest person can acquire money. One is to work for it. The second is to accept handouts: welfare, unemployment, or an allowance from relatives. The third is to let your money earn more for you.

Living on handouts is the last thing most of us want to consider. To avoid this, we're trained from the time we start school to aim for a good job. Parents and other relatives, teachers, and career counselors all join to convince us our financial security lies in getting and keeping the best job we're capable of learning.

Just how well will we do if we follow this advice? Look at the following list of the twenty highest-paid jobs in the United States and their average salaries, along with a description of the education needed to qualify for those jobs. Clearly, large numbers of people could never complete the training for many of these positions, for a variety of reasons.

TWENTY HIGHEST-PAID JOBS IN THE UNITED STATES

PROFESSION AND PREPARATION	AVERAGE ANNUAL INCOME
SURGEON	$164,724
3–4 YRS. COLLEGE, BACHELOR'S DEGREE	
4 YRS. MEDICAL SCHOOL	
3–8 YRS. ADVANCED TRAINING	

PSYCHIATRIST $ 93,916
    4 YRS. COLLEGE
    4 YRS. MEDICAL SCHOOL
    1–5 YRS. ADVANCED TRAINING

OSTEOPATH $ 87,200
    3–4 YRS. COLLEGE, BACHELOR'S DEGREE
    4 YRS. MEDICAL SCHOOL
    1–3 YRS. ADVANCED TRAINING

CHIROPRACTOR $ 72,267
    2–4 YRS. UNDERGRADUATE STUDY
    4 YRS. CHIROPRACTIC COLLEGE

DENTIST $ 65,400
    3–4 YRS. COLLEGE
    4 YRS. DENTAL SCHOOL

ORTHODONTIST $ 65,400
    3–4 YRS. COLLEGE
    4 YRS. DENTAL SCHOOL
    2–4 YRS. POSTGRADUATE TRAINING

VETERINARIAN $ 50,140
    2 YRS. PREVETERINARY COLLEGE COURSES
    4 YRS. COLLEGE OF VETERINARY MEDICINE

AEROSPACE ENGINEER $ 44,680
    4 YRS. COLLEGE
    1–5 YRS. GRADUATE SCHOOL FOR BETTER-
    PAYING JOBS

CIVIL ENGINEER $ 44,680
    4 YRS. COLLEGE
    1–5 YRS. GRADUATE SCHOOL

ATTORNEY $ 43,474
    4 YRS. COLLEGE
    3 YRS. LAW SCHOOL

INDUSTRIAL ENGINEER $ 43,450
    4 YRS. COLLEGE
    2–4 YRS. GRADUATE SCHOOL

MECHANICAL ENGINEER $ 43,450
    4 YRS. COLLEGE
    1–5 YRS. GRADUATE SCHOOL

ELECTRICAL ENGINEER $ 43,450
    4 YRS. COLLEGE
    2–4 YRS. GRADUATE SCHOOL

PSYCHOLOGIST $ 43,382
    4 YRS. COLLEGE
    3–5 YRS. GRADUATE STUDY
    1–2 YRS. INTERNSHIP
ARCHITECT $ 38,804
    4 YRS. COLLEGE
    1–3 YRS. ADDITIONAL SCHOOL AND/OR EXPE-
    RIENCE UNDER A REGISTERED ARCHITECT
ACCOUNTANT $ 35,098
    4 YRS. COLLEGE
    1–2 YRS. ADDITIONAL SCHOOLING AND/OR EX-
    PERIENCE
COMMISSIONED OFFICER $ 34,391
    4 YRS. COLLEGE, PLUS 2–5 HRS. PER WEEK OF
    ROTC FOR THOSE NOT ATTENDING A MILITARY
    COLLEGE
OPTOMETRIST $ 34,444
    2–3 YRS. COLLEGE
    4 YRS. OPTOMETRIC SCHOOL OR COLLEGE
PHARMACIST $ 32,264
    MINIMUM 5 YRS. TRAINING, TO INCLUDE
    1–2 YRS. COLLEGE
    3–4 YRS. PHARMACY SCHOOL
REGISTERED NURSE $ 26,073
    2–5 YRS. TRAINING IN 2–YR. COLLEGE, TEACH-
    ING HOSPITAL, AND/OR COLLEGE OR UNIVER-
    SITY

INFORMATION DERIVED FROM *THE JOBS RATED ALMANAC*, EDITED BY LES KRANTZ, AMERICAN REFERENCES INC., CHICAGO, 1988, AND *OCCUPATIONAL OUTLOOK HANDBOOK 1988–89 EDITION*, U.S. DEPARTMENT OF LABOR BUREAU OF LABOR STATISTICS, WASHINGTON, D.C., 1988.

Every one of these professions requires special talents and abilities: mathematical aptitude for accountants and engineers, specialized training for medical and military careers, and so on. In addition, they all call for large commitments of time and tens of thousands of dollars to complete the training. Many of us who have the skills don't have the opportunity to educate ourselves for these jobs.

17

Even if we have one of these highly paid jobs, do they truly lead to financial independence? No, not usually. Most people spend everything they earn, and often more, on their ordinary living expenses. In addition, having a good job is no guarantee that you won't lose it. Between mergers, hostile takeovers, new technologies, and an uncertain economy, very few jobs can be considered safe, lifetime employment anymore. Many white-collar managers are no more secure today than the average factory worker was during the Great Depression of the 1930s.

A few people manage to save something or to start a small investment program during their working lives. The majority of the working population, however—95 percent—reaches retirement with nothing to fall back on but Social Security benefits. That's practically the same as living on handouts.

True, they have worked for their benefits, so it's not exactly the same as outright charity. The effect is much the same, though. They receive a monthly allowance, and for most people it's not enough to live comfortably. They must either seek help from relatives or supplemental welfare programs or do without things they need and want.

What sort of way is that to live? Why spend your most productive years working for someone else, always in danger of losing your livelihood, and then end your life scraping by on an inadequate pension? It doesn't have to be that way, and I'm going to show you ways to avoid it.

The real key to financial security is not in holding a good job, but in learning to make your money work for you, and I'm going to tell you how to do it. There are several different ways to take advantage of this information. You can use it to save money on almost everything you buy, including clothes, appliances, luxury items such as clothes and jewelry, and even automobiles, boats, and houses.

How much money can you save? You may have some trouble believing this, but with the special techniques I'm going to show you, you can often buy these items as cheaply as ten cents on the dollar.

This means you can take enormous discounts on almost every-

18

thing you buy for yourself. If you like, you can enjoy a more luxurious life-style on the same income you earn now and still put away some of the money you save as an extra retirement fund for yourself. That's the most conservative approach, but I've got some even better ideas for you.

For one thing, you can use your savings as capital to start one or more small businesses—depending on your own interests and market opportunities. This will generate extra income and give you something to fall back on in case you lose your regular job. Of course, if you don't have a job at all, many of these ideas can be used to lift you out of the ranks of the unemployed and start earning returns almost immediately.

Finally, the most lucrative use of the money you save by following my suggestions is to start an investment plan for yourself. I'll tell you what to buy, and how, so that your money earns more for you. Once you get started on this plan, there's no limit to how far you can go. Many of my students have retired in their thirties and forties on handsome incomes generated by their investments.

IT'S NOT COMPLICATED

The information you'll read in these pages is drawn from the Cash Flow System course I've taught to thousands of people over the past seven years. "Cash flow" is a financial term applied to the way money moves and can be positive, negative, balanced, or zero. When an individual or business makes a profit—that is, has more money coming in than going out—it's called positive cash flow; negative cash flow means less money comes in than goes out, resulting in a loss. Balanced cash flow describes the situation where income exactly balances outgo, while zero cash flow means money is neither received nor spent.

My Cash Flow System teaches people how, starting from whatever economic position they occupy, they can generate or increase their positive cash flow and then how they can expand that income stream to the level they desire. One of the best features of the Cash Flow System is that it's not complicated. I'm not going to tell you it doesn't take some work, because it does; everything worthwhile in this life takes a certain amount of effort and concentration. But the Cash Flow System can be understood and put into practice by almost anyone. You don't need a college degree, or even a high school diploma, to use this system. My successful students include people from all educational levels, including high school dropouts.

One of the most rewarding things about teaching the Cash Flow System has been the variety of people who have been helped by it and their joy in what they've accomplished. I've had the privilege of interviewing some of them for my nationally syndicated television show, and they're wonderful people. The young blind boy who uses part of his investment profits to help blind children was one of my favorite guests. It was great to hear the former bricklayer whose back problems kept him from his trade talk about the life he and his family enjoyed once they put the Cash Flow System to work for them; or the many divorced women who learned how to support their families; or the man from Los Angeles who uses my concepts to show teenagers they don't have to steal or be involved in drugs to get what they want from life.

$$ MONEYMAKER $$

Don't worry about starting with less than nothing. Tom Monaghan grew up as a foster child and was expelled from the tenth grade for bad behavior. Looking for a way to support himself and finish his education, he borrowed $500 and traded a Volkswagen to gain control of a small pizza business.

The business took so much time, Monaghan dropped out of school again. Trying to make his operation stand out from every other small pizza place, Tom concentrated on fast deliveries. He offered a guarantee: If you don't receive your pizza within thirty minutes, you keep the pizza and pay nothing.

His imagination and hard work paid off, making Domino's the second-largest pizza company after Pizza Hut and Tom one of the four hundred richest Americans. In addition to real estate, he now owns the Detroit Tigers baseball team and a classic car collection and is estimated to have a net worth of $300 million. The point is, you don't have to dream up a new product, or even a better product, to succeed. Often, all you need is better packaging, a better service, or a better way to fill an existing need.

Those are some of my rewards. What rewards do you want? A better life-style? Increased income? Financial independence? The opportunity to help someone else? It's up to you. We all have different dreams and ambitions, which gives life its variety. But whatever your dream is, I can show you how to turn it into reality. Then it's up to you to make it happen.

SUCCESS IS IN YOUR HANDS

I will provide you with a variety of plans for reaching your financial goals. You can use every idea or plan or pick and choose the ones you like most and that apply best to your current situation. If you have little or no cash, you'll find suggestions for raising capital and finding partners. You'll learn how, once you've used those ideas to produce some funds, you can multiply your holdings to whatever level you desire. Those of you who already have some money put by will learn ways to use it to generate better returns than you can find in any savings plan and much more safely than investing it in the stock market.

$$ MONEYMAKER $$

Your hobby could generate extra cash. If you produce anything—crafts, furniture, photographs, animals, clothing, and so on—you could offer some for sale or custom-design specialty items. You might teach classes for beginners who want to learn your hobby. You could specialize in accessories for others who share your interest: hand-painted cars and scenery for model railroads, mats and frames for paintings, handy tool caddies for gardeners, and so on. Many people have turned their hobbies into rewarding full-time businesses. Debbie Fields did it with Mrs. Fields cookies, which grew out of the compliments her friends gave her over her "soft" baked cookies. Her baking hobby has now become a multimillion-dollar nationwide company.

Ease in with a minimal investment just to test the waters, and remember that you can often accomplish more with imaginative free publicity than by spending hard-earned dollars on advertising. You might begin by offering a free seminar or class on the subject at a school and arranging for your local newspaper to cover the event.

Your success will depend on more than having a plan to follow, however. You'll also need the discipline to apply yourself. It's up to you to study the techniques I will describe until you understand them, then go out into the world and put them into practice. If you want to reach the ultimate goal of financial independence, you can't make excuses to put off the day when you'll actually start working on your plan. No one ever excused his way to success.

I know that it's sometimes difficult, and even frightening, to try new things and change your way of life. That's why, if you truly want to succeed, you must discipline yourself to work through your plan. Others have done it, and so can you. Simply take it one step at a time, at your own pace. Once you've accomplished one step, go on to the next; don't back off and lose your momentum.

This discipline factor is so important to achieving anything you want in life that I've incorporated it into a formula that I use as a motto for my Cash Flow System students:

$$Plan + Discipline = Success$$

CHAPTER 2

Ten Keys to Financial Power

If you've never managed a financial enterprise of your own before, the kind of discipline you'll need to follow your particular plan may be new to you. Or you may never have sat down and consciously thought about it before. Let's look at some of the characteristics you can develop that will make you more successful in anything you try.

Successful people share certain common attributes. Some people learn how to achieve what they want during childhood, while others wait until they're grown to develop success-oriented behavior. This makes it clear that these traits are not inborn, but can be learned. If you want success, you'll memorize these characteristics and do everything you can to develop them in yourself.

The first requirement for success, of course, is to have a goal—something you want to achieve, a point you wish to reach, whether it's a dollar amount of money, a tangible item you want to possess, or a particular level of skill you desire to reach in some activity.

The best goals are the most concrete, and I advise you to write down an exact description of what you want in the most specific terms possible. If you want cash, don't just record your goal as "more money," but choose the exact amount you desire. You might write "an income of $500,000 a year" or "a net worth of $3,000,000." Instead of saying, "I want a better car," describe it exactly: "I want a red Mercedes convertible with black upholstery.'' If possible, find a picture of what you want and pin it up where you'll see it several times a day. Rather than wishing you knew how to make more money, start with, ''I'm going to learn how to generate $500 [or $5,000] a month in additional income.''

Next, set yourself a reasonable time limit for what you want to accomplish. Break your goal down into individual steps, the small milestones that mark your progress toward your ultimate target, and set dates for the completion of each step. Write all this down and review your progress at regular intervals, revising your targets and timetable as necessary.

Now, assuming you have a goal, what characteristics should you develop and practice so you can reach that goal? Here are the ten that have been found in common among successful people in all fields.

1. Motivated. You must want to reach your goal more than anything else. Working toward it must become the most important activity in your life—more important than watching television, socializing with friends, or keeping up with the latest books and movies.

Naturally, when you have family or other important people in your life, you can't always expect them to take a backseat to your ambitions. Often, though, you can convince them to join you in your interests. Even when you can't, you'll want to spend some time with them in mutually enjoyable activities.

I'm not suggesting you cut everyone and everything else out of your life. But you must set priorities and make choices. Decide what's most important in your life, and eliminate unnecessary pastimes that take away energy and time you could use to work toward your goal.

2. Action-oriented. True achievers reduce daydreaming and useless activities. Instead of dwelling on fantasies of how wonderful life could be when they reach their goals, these people invest their time and efforts in active work to help them achieve what they want.

Notice, I said they *reduce* their daydreaming. They don't eliminate it altogether. An active imagination can be an asset in finding creative ways to achieve what you want. Also, a certain amount of fantasizing about your future goal helps keep your motivation fresh.

24

But when you spend too much time envisioning the future, and not enough working in the present, you'll never get anywhere.

If you find your mind wandering during the time you've set aside to work toward your goal, allow yourself a short break, perhaps five or ten minutes every couple of hours, to imagine the fulfillment of your dreams. Then get back to work to make those dreams come true.

3. Healthy. In order to be your most productive, you have to keep yourself in the best possible mental and physical condition. There's no point in succumbing to stress or the effects of overwork in pursuit of your goal. How will you enjoy your success if you become ill achieving it?

Not all of us are blessed with perfect bodies, of course, and there's no point straining to become Jane Fonda or Arnold Schwarzenegger if you're not built that way. Learn your own personal most desirable weight and fitness level, probably through a visit with your doctor, and adopt a reasonable diet and exercise plan. Get enough rest and maintain a cheerful, positive mental outlook. After all, becoming wealthy is one of the most rewarding things that can happen to us in life.

4. Independent. Successful people recognize that they are responsible for every step of their achievements. You must be able to work alone, if necessary, on every task toward your goal.

This doesn't mean that you must do all your own accounting, or legal work, or any other specialized job. But it does mean that you're responsible for seeing that it's done, and done competently, by someone who is qualified to perform the necessary tasks. You're a self-starter, ready and able to get going on whatever needs to be done next. You recognize when jobs require your attention, and don't need someone to give you permission to act or to nag you into performing.

You can direct others when it is necessary. You take charge every step of the way. If others don't approve of what you're doing, you'll listen to their objections, of course. You'll also listen to the advice of experts. But you'll make the final decisions for yourself.

5. Flexible. Accepting and adapting to changing conditions is an important part of success. Times change, and so do people and

25

━━━━━ **$$ MONEYMAKER $$** ━━━━━

Early in your success program, start putting together a winning team, a support group to help you reach your goals. Surround yourself with positive, optimistic people who help you celebrate your achievements and cheer you when you're discouraged. Gather names of competent, reliable attorneys, accountants, and other experts you might consult, and interview them so you'll know whom to turn to when you need advice.

To find candidates for your personal team of expert advisers, ask others who are active in the field that interests you. For instance, if you want to market an invention, you might attend an inventors' convention and talk to as many attendees as you can, particularly those who have already achieved some success. Admit your ignorance and ask who helped them with financing, filing patents, and other details. Then ask if they were pleased with the help they received or if they think someone else would have done a better job.

When you collect names of three or four people who receive good recommendations, interview these people. Describe what you want to accomplish and the assistance you require from them, and evaluate their answers. Look for those who understand you and your goals and who display a broad knowledge of the field and a confident attitude.

their needs. Economic situations fluctuate, markets shift, new trends emerge as old ones die out. What worked last year, or last week, may be disastrous tomorrow, as many blacksmiths and livery stable owners learned when the automobile became popular in the early days of this century. Those who thought of themselves as part of the transportation industry moved with the times, installing gasoline pumps and learning to repair engines. They prospered while competitors who believed they were in the horse business complained about hard times and looked for other work.

For a more recent example, look at the way certain fast-food chains have changed in the last few years. McDonald's and Burger King rose to success with hamburgers, but in the 1980s Americans became more concerned with their diets. Today the big names in hamburgers include fish, chicken, and salads on their menus.

You can't jump from one endeavor to the next so quickly that your plans don't have time to mature or projects begin to deliver their profits. You need enough patience to let profitable enterprises develop. However, you shouldn't become so stuck on one thing, whether it's a particular business or investment, a location, a type of partnership, a contract form, or anything else, that you continue to follow outmoded patterns when they no longer work. Be open to new ideas, and if they prove more promising than your old ones, be willing to try them out.

6. Determined.   Don't give up on a good idea because of temporary problems or a lack of faith from others. We all encounter obstacles; nothing in this world is perfect, and things never go smoothly all the time. Realize this before you start anything, and resolve to find solutions to your problems and ways around obstacles.

As for a lack of faith from others, years ago a woman named Evelyn E. Smith said, ''When you discover something new, everybody thinks you're crazy.'' Think of all the people in history who would agree with that statement! Probably the first person to make a wheel was regarded as the tribe mental case. Do you remember hearing about Fulton's Folly in school? That's what they called the steamboat Robert Fulton invented, until it proved a success.

I could go on and on about lack of faith: music teachers called the young Ludwig van Beethoven ''hopeless''; the telephone, the automobile, and the airplane were all regarded as useless toys by most of the people who saw the first models; dozens of the most famous inventors, writers, and actors were told they should take up other lines of work. You can probably think of a few examples of your own.

The point is, most people won't believe you can do something until you go ahead and do it. Make up your mind from the start that you are the only one who can decide what you can or cannot do, and let nothing stand in the way of achieving what you want.

7. Decisive.   Some people hate to make any decision, ever. Others spend so much time and effort worrying about past decisions that they drain all their energy in useless fretting.

Successful people avoid both these extremes. They gather as much information as they can before they have to decide a question. If that's a lot of information, fine; if it's only a little, they do the best they can. Based on whatever they can learn, they make the best decision they can at that moment and then move on to the next task.

Naturally, you'll want to make informed decisions whenever you can. But sometimes it's simply not possible. If it makes you feel better, you can remind yourself to go back and review the decision at a later date, when you have more information. In some cases that's vital, but more often it's not. Usually the most important move is to make some decision and act on it, even if occasionally your decision is to do nothing about the matter and move on to something else.

8. Confident. A belief in yourself and your ideas is vital to your success. It's what keeps you going when others question your judgment, your ability, and your sanity. It's also important in persuading others to follow your directions and your ideas.

Your belief and enthusiasm will convince others to loan you money or invest in projects with you. And as we'll see later, persuading others can be a vital ingredient in your plan to reach financial independence.

Developing confidence can seem like a difficult job to some people. It's really fairly simple, but takes some practice. The basic ingredient is knowledge. When you know and understand what you're doing, you can't help but be confident. Study what you plan to do until you're sure you understand it, and ask questions of anyone who might be able to give you good advice. The more you know, the more confident you'll feel.

9. Thrifty. The most successful financial achievers spend money only where necessary for the success of their enterprises, at least until their profits can support a few extras. It makes no sense to take money out of an investment program, for example, to rent luxury offices if you don't need to invest from a fancy office.

One of the saddest examples of this I ever saw was a man who ran a small mail-order business. One month he placed an ad in a national magazine and received ten times the volume of orders he had expected. It was the first time he'd ever seen so much money, and he got so excited, he ran out and bought an expensive boat instead of putting the money back into more advertising and greater capability to handle the increased volume of orders. He repeated this pattern of self-indulgence until he lost his business.

Before spending any money, financially successful people ask themselves two questions: 1) Do I really need this? 2) Where could the money be put to better use? They weigh the answers to these questions very carefully before deciding to commit money to any unnecessary expenses. You don't have to become a total tightwad to be successful. But you must budget your money as carefully as you do your time, particularly in the early stages of your success program.

10. Informed. Success depends on knowing what goes on in the world and how it affects your interests. You have to be alert to new trends and shifts in the marketplace if you're going to stay ahead of the competition. You can collect information from all kinds of sources: newspapers, trade journals and newsletters, books, seminars, computer data banks, and contacts with people who share your concerns. In fact, these days we're said to live in an "information age" where we're practically buried in news, facts, and rumors.

That's why it's important to be selective about your information

---

$$ MONEYMAKER $$

When you need office space but can't quite afford it, look for someone else in the same position and share an office. Or find an existing business that doesn't need all its space and ask to use part of that office. Or lease more space than you need, then sublease some of it to another business.

Rent out unused rooms as storage space. Offer mailing services in addition to your regular business: postal boxes, UPS, and express mail pickup and delivery. (Sell stamps, envelopes, wrapping paper, tape, and other supplies.) Offer copying and fax service. Run courier, secretarial, and telephone answering services from your office— either hire the people and direct the business yourself, or let people who want to start these businesses operate from your address.

Rent your entire space during nonbusiness hours to another operation, or start one yourself: tutoring, computer training, hobby classes, counseling services, evening telemarketing or collection operations, part-time tax and accounting services, small seminars and meetings, and so on. Talk to people in your community for ideas on needed services and think about how you could accommodate one or more of them.

---

gathering. If you don't make choices, it's all too easy to spend most of your time reading, attending lectures and meetings, and networking. You can find you have little or no time left to do any actual work toward your goal; worse yet, you may become so overloaded with information, some of it contradictory, that you can't decide what to do.

When you're first learning about a new interest, it's wise to sample as many information sources as you can. Get a feel for what each one has to offer and how well it suits you and your needs. Does it present the facts in a way you understand? Does it deal directly with your central interests, or is it concerned mainly with matters you don't need to think about, at least for now?

People's needs vary, depending on what financial avenues they follow. In general, though, once they're familiar with their field, most people should keep informed in the following ways:

- A daily newspaper that gives you local news that might affect your dealings
- A daily newscast that keeps you up to date on national and world events that could influence your business
- One to three weekly or monthly trade journals and newsletters bringing you developments and analyses concerning your interests
- Conversations at least once a month, and preferably once a week, with others who have information to share about your field
- A class, seminar, or convention once or twice a year to update your knowledge and introduce you to new developments

In addition to these, you might plug into a computer data-base service once every couple of weeks if you find one that offers material you can use. Your trade journals and personal contacts will also alert you to worthwhile books or even videotapes. Being in the education business, I'm tempted to recommend you study at least one of these every month; but since I'm also a realist, I'm forced to admit that two a year is a more manageable number.

If you're not used to keeping up with a profession, you may

think that's an incredible amount of material for one person to wade through every month. However, I'm not suggesting you should read or listen to every word from each source. You do need to skim, though, and select those items that appear to have an impact on what you want to do.

Also, you'll find that some ways of keeping informed can be combined with or substituted for other activities. You can listen to the news while you get ready for work or fix a meal, or skim magazines and newsletters instead of spending an evening in front of the television. Many books and courses are available on audio cassettes, which you might listen to as you drive around on errands or take your daily exercise.

There you have it. Those are the ten behavior patterns common to most successful people in every field. I've summarized them all in the list below.

TEN TRAITS OF SUCCESSFUL PERSONALITIES

1. **Motivated.** Want to reach your goal more than anything else.
2. **Action-oriented.** Invest time in working toward your goal, not in daydreaming or useless activities.
3. **Healthy.** Keep yourself in your best possible mental and physical condition.
4. **Independent.** Realize you are responsible for every step of your success and be able to work alone, if necessary, on every task toward your goal.
5. **Flexible.** Accept and adapt to changing conditions.
6. **Determined.** Don't give up on a good idea because of temporary problems or lack of faith from others.
7. **Decisive.** Make the best choice available with the information you have, then go on to the next task.
8. **Confident.** Believe in yourself and your ideas; use your belief and enthusiasm to persuade others.
9. **Thrifty.** Spend money only where necessary for the success of your enterprise until profits can support frills.

31

10. Informed. Know what's going on and how it affects your business.

To develop these characteristics in yourself, take them one at a time. Practice the one you've chosen until it becomes a habit. Once you've incorporated one new habit into your life, start on the next one, and soon you'll develop a more success-oriented personality. It's that personality that will translate my techniques for achieving financial independence into reality.

CHAPTER **3**

Buying Far Below Market Value

The first benefit you can enjoy from the Cash Flow System, and the one that interests many people initially, is the way you can cut expenses on a variety of merchandise you buy for yourself. Jackets and jeans, blankets, golf clubs, television and stereo equipment, dishes, lamps, and cookware are only the beginning. Everything from beds to bicycles, handbags to hot tubs, and water wings to welding torches are available, all over the country, at a fraction of their retail cost.

These bargains aren't limited to small household items, either. You can buy airplanes, boats, and automobiles, office equipment such as desks, computers, file cabinets, copy machines, and typewriters, and even luxury goods such as jewelry and furs. Real estate of all kinds is available at low prices, often with favorable financing (and I'll show you some creative ways anyone can use to buy real estate when financing is not readily available or is simply too expensive).

You can find real bargains in a wide variety of purchases you might buy for yourself and your family, from clothes to a new home. As a result, your normal living expenses will decline, and with the money you save you might buy higher-quality goods or a few extras you couldn't afford before. You could even save money toward your retirement.

BUY LOW TO SELL HIGH

My advice, though, is to take advantage of bargain prices to buy low and sell high. With your profits, you can purchase more items to sell to others, and as your earnings continue to grow, you can set aside part of them to acquire income-producing investments. When you follow this plan, you're working yourself into the position where your money earns more money for you with little or no effort on your part. You are well on the way to reaching your goal of becoming financially independent.

Now let's focus on the specific key to making this happen. How can you buy practically anything at ridiculously low prices? In one word, the answer is *auctions*.

Yes, truly. There is much more to auctions than furniture sales and bidding on high-priced art. From local sales to auctions sponsored by the federal government, the opportunities for savings and profit are practically unlimited. Just to illustrate, let me give you a few true examples.

A woman in Los Angeles bought an airplane at a U.S. Customs Service auction for $15,000, then turned around and sold it for $90,000. Since the plane's market value was well over $100,000, the final buyer still got a good deal, while the auction buyer made a fantastic profit.

A San Francisco man bought a $700 fur jacket for $200 during a U.S. Postal Service auction. He had a lot of trouble deciding whether to sell it to someone else for $500 or just to give it to his wife as a gift.

Then there was the lawyer from Georgia who bought a property at auction for unpaid back taxes in South Carolina. He paid $9,500 for a forty-acre ranch. The ranch included a 3,500-square-foot house, a swimming pool with bathhouse, a two-car garage, a kennel, and an outbuilding. The ranch was appraised at a value of $122,700.

Also in South Carolina, a Lincoln Continental, a Mercedes-Benz, a van, furniture, silver flatware, and a television set were sold at auction as one lot, for a total price of $17,500. Have you priced a Mercedes lately?

If you aren't into expensive cars, how about motorcycles at

prices from $25 to $250? That was the range at an auction in New York. Or for something in between, would you pay $1,100 for a Chevy van only three years old? That went in New York also, along with over a hundred other autos. Many went as cheaply as $100 apiece. Some of the cheaper ones weren't in running condition; but you can sell the parts from almost any car for more than $100 and put cash in your pocket.

And those are just a few items offered at auctions. I've seen people pay $25 for rings valued at over $200 and buy jewelry worth over $2,500 for under $1,000. I saw Lalique porcelain figures normally priced from $175 to $225 auctioned off at prices ranging from $25 to $75. I've seen brand-new clothing, never worn, sold in lots of assorted sizes for 10 percent of its value, including sweaters, sports coats, jeans, dresses, baby clothes, coats, and even under-wear. The buyers generally keep what fits them and their families and sell the rest at a profit.

None of these auction bargains is particularly rare. I only mention them because they happen to stick in my mind. The people who bought the items were so excited, or I was so surprised at how few people bid, that I recall these bargains more easily than others. But buys like these are made all over the country all the time. And you can be a buyer.

LEARN THE BASICS

There are techniques to profiting from auctions and certain kinds of auctions where your opportunities are better than at others. You need

---

— $$ MONEYMAKER $$ —

In San Francisco a large corporation closed down its regional head-quarters and auctioned off the contents of a block-long, seven-story office building. One man bought over a hundred metal desks for $5 to $10 apiece. He planned to sell them to a store that specializes in used office equipment and pays its suppliers an average of $35 per desk. On a hundred desks, with an average price of $7.50 each, that was a profit of $2,750 for a morning's work—and the store even sent its own truck to pick up the desks.

---

to know more about these things before you actually go out and take part in an auction.

This information isn't secret, although most of it is unfamiliar to the general public. Most of the various auctions and sales we'll discuss are held in every city in the country. The rest are easily accessible to anyone who's determined to increase his or her cash flow. If you examine past records for your city, you'll learn that informed people have been making money through these channels for years.

You don't have to worry, though, that now these ideas are being published, the competition will make it impossible for you to profit. For one thing, not everyone who learns these techniques will go out and put them to work. Others will lose their motivation or get sidetracked into more comfortable, familiar activities than building their fortunes. Only a few of you—those who really want your success plans to work and are willing to step out of your ruts and take a little extra effort to build financial independence—will stick to these ideas and use them as a springboard to increased earnings and investment power.

BASIC AUCTION STRATEGIES

The best way to discover the world of auctions is to visit a variety of local auction sales. These are not the more specialized sales I'll be describing later, but they are a good place to start. Auction houses vary greatly in their size and scope and in the kinds of items they offer. Some houses deal only in antiques. Others work strictly with estate sales. Others handle only farm equipment. The best way to find out in advance what sort of merchandise will be offered at a particular sale is to check out your local auction houses and read auction notices in your local newspaper.

Local auction notices are usually published in their own section of the classified ads of the newspaper. Check out the Saturday and Sunday papers for the greatest range of sales. Also, look in your local Yellow Pages under *Auctioneers*. Most auction houses welcome telephone inquiries and will be glad to put you on their mailing lists to notify you of future sales.

It's also a good idea to get into the habit of looking at the Legal Notices section of your local paper on a regular basis. Since the law often requires a legal notice to be published before a seller can dispose of personal property, you can learn about many private and government sales this way. Check with your county clerk for a list of newspapers that run legal notices in your area.

How Auctions Differ from Retail Sales

Purchasing at auctions is very different from buying at most retail outlets. Here are some of the basic differences between auction buying and purchasing the same type of item from your local store:

1. **Price.** At a store, the price of an item is fixed. If you feel that the price is too high, you can shop around or settle for lesser quality at a lower price.

    Auction prices evolve. As a bidder, you participate in setting the price. Sometimes the sellers set a minimum price for an item, below which they will not go. At other times there is *no set price*—which means that you may well have the opportunity to create a great bargain!

2. **Quality of merchandise.** At a store, unless it's a second-hand store, the items you purchase are new and unused. If you discover a flaw, you have the option to return or exchange anything you buy.

    Auction items are sometimes used or secondhand. Because every bidder is given the opportunity to inspect the items before the sale, everything is sold "as is." If you discover a flaw in an item after you've purchased it, it's your loss. You have to fix it yourself or live with it. For this reason, close inspections and a good knowledge of your prospective purchases are essential.

3. **Payment and delivery.** At a store, you can often pay for your purchases in cash, by check, or with a credit card or some sort of in-house credit plan. If you can't take your purchase with you immediately, many stores will arrange delivery for you for a small fee.

At an auction, the full price of the item is usually due immediately, or at most within a day or two. Rules for payment vary greatly between different auction houses. Some houses demand cash only; others will take personal checks if you've established a line of credit. Bidding is open to anyone who wanders into some auction houses; others require a minimum deposit from anyone who wants to participate. This deposit is deducted from the money you owe for an item if you make a winning bid; if you don't make any winning bids, your deposit is refunded to you at the end of the auction.

There are also no set rules for delivery of the items you purchase. In general, once you conclude the sale, the item is yours, and it's your responsibility to make delivery arrangements. Some auction houses have connections with delivery companies, which can wind up saving you money; but this varies from house to house.

Learning Your Way Around Auctions

The best way to learn about auctions is to attend them. If you've never bought at an auction before, visit a few local auctions just to look around.

Most auctions hold previews to show their items to the public and to give everyone a chance to inspect the merchandise before the bidding starts. A preview may last for an entire day or more and be held any time up to the day before the auction; or it may last for only an hour or two and be held on sale day before the bidding starts. These previews usually don't require a deposit and are open to the general public.

When you first enter the viewing area, look around carefully. You should find a list, known as the sale list or catalog, of the items up for auction. If you don't find this catalog, search out someone in charge and ask for it.

The catalog names the items up for sale, gives each one a lot number, and sometimes lists a minimum bid. Sometimes, too, the catalog lists an "estimated value" or "appraised value" for merchandise, which is there simply for your information. At some sales these values are accurate, while at others they seem less exact; it all depends on who does the appraisal. Never let these estimates substitute for your own knowledge of an item's value, and don't worry too much about them. When it comes to bidding, estimates and appraisals usually have very little connection with the actual sale price.

Take your time at the preview. Shop around. Inspect the items closely. Try to get an idea of what *you* think a particular item is worth; then compare that price with the minimum bid (if there is one). Write down your own estimate of the highest price you'd be willing to pay for anything you're interested in.

After you've seen the preview, attend the auction. Don't put yourself under any particular pressure to buy. Tell yourself that you're there to learn and to acquire a new skill.

Generally, the first thing you'll notice about most auctions is the air of repressed excitement in the room. People whisper to each other and glance around, eyeing the bargains they're most anxious to bid on and wondering if anyone will bid against them. In a way, it reminds me of the beginning of the first dance at a junior high school. Everyone is waiting for something wonderful to happen and hoping it will happen to them.

When the bidding actually starts, the excitement increases. Things move fast. Lots—which can be anything from a single item to a large assortment of unrelated merchandise—may be brought up to the front of the room or their numbers simply called out with a short description of what the lot contains. As the items people have been waiting for go on the block, the bidders become more and more enthusiastic. Then, when they've bid on what they wanted and won the bid, they feel victorious. Finally, when it's all over and people are picking up their purchases, the room hums with happy exclamations as buyers smile and compare notes on their bargains.

The funny thing is, this happens even when there are few bidders present and many articles go unsold for lack of interest. The people who are there enjoy it just as much as when the room is packed. The enthusiasm and excitement are great, but you have to learn to guard against these feelings. Old pros call it "auction fever." That's when people get so carried away that they bid on anything and everything, with no regard to its true value. Amateurs can bid an item up beyond its retail price or end up buying something they have absolutely no use for, simply because they get caught up in the fun or give in to their competitive spirit.

Auction fever has no place in plans to use auctions as a source of low-priced investment merchandise or bargains on personal possessions. That's why I advise everyone to visit the auction preview and make careful estimates of their highest bids beforehand and then stick to those figures.

Of course, when you're visiting auctions to learn about them and you see an item you like, you're as free to bid as anyone, as long as you offer only what you think an item is worth. If someone outbids you, you've still learned something. You've had the chance to see how realistic your original estimate was, you've gotten acquainted with the location, you've learned how many other people show up, and you've seen the bidding process in action. You're that much closer to success. With practice your predictions will get more accurate, and you'll feel more confident of your judgment on future purchases.

AUCTION SUCCESS TAKES PRACTICE

Just like any other valuable skill that I can think of, learning to buy at auctions is something that develops with time and practice. Don't expect yourself to know everything immediately, *and don't give up*! If you go to only one or two auctions, you may not see anything you think you want to buy. Or you may decide on purchasing a few items, only to find that other people are willing to bid more money for them than you are. This is the time to increase your efforts, attend more auctions, bid on more items, and turn your knowledge and energy into increased cash flow.

Now, before we get into the cash flow opportunities explained in the rest of this book, there's something else you should know: how to buy successfully at an auction. I have a set of rules for this, which I call my "Auction Success Formula."

```
╔══════════ $$ MONEYMAKER $$ ══════════╗
║ When you plan to bid on high-ticket items at auction, line up credit  ║
║ in advance so you're ready to move when an opportunity appears.       ║
║ Homeowners could borrow on a home equity loan (HEL), then hold        ║
║ the money in a special interest-earning investment account until time ║
║ to buy. Alternatively, save the interest payments on your loan by     ║
║ simply not drawing out the money until you need it for the auction.   ║
╚═══════════════════════════════════════╝
```

AUCTION SUCCESS FORMULA

1. **Decide on the top price you'll pay before the bidding starts.**
   a. Figure the asset's market value and fast sale value.
   b. Refuse to bid more than your top price.
2. **Have a plan in mind for what you buy.**
   a. Estimate your monetary gain plus the amount of effort it will take to sell at a profit.
   b. Make a list of likely buyers.
3. **If you don't have enough money to bid on an item, form a partnership with another person or group of people.**

Do Your Homework

Becoming a skilled auction buyer means acquiring knowledge and doing your homework. Before an auction even starts, you should know what kinds of items you're going to bid on and what kinds of prices those items usually bring.

If you're going to bid on handmade Oriental rugs, for example, you should know what qualities to look for in these rugs. How do you tell if one is in good condition? How does size affect price? What about age, color, texture, or national origin? Is the market for Oriental rugs going up or down? If rugs interest you, it's worth your while to do your research before you even arrive at a sale.

For this reason, I recommend starting out with items that already interest you. If you like rugs, for example, chances are you already know a lot about rug prices to begin with. Plus it's always enjoyable to learn more about something you're interested in.

41

How do you start your research? There are several ways to find what you need to know about virtually any subject. Check with your local library. Chances are good that your librarian can come up with books or newsletters that deal directly with your area of interest. Museums and retail stores can be good sources of information. Local colleges and universities offer courses in many fields and might have a class that's directly suited to your interest. And, of course, just by attending auctions you'll meet other people who share your interests. Get to know them. You'll find new friends and possibly even partners. The more you read and observe, the more you'll learn about your field of interest.

As your experience increases, you'll become better able to make accurate assessments of the values of items you see at auction. You'll be able to decide what an item is really worth—and the maximum price you can bid and still make a profit.

KNOWLEDGE PAYS OFF OVER AND OVER

Learning how to resell goods you've bought at an auction is another skill you'll acquire as you learn how to make the Cash Flow System work for you. We'll talk more about this later on, since it's not a skill that's valuable only in reselling auction goods. You'll use the knowledge you gain selling smaller items when it comes time to resell the more profitable investment vehicles, such as real estate, that you buy.

Just as you research value before you buy, you can research where likely markets are and who will be interested when you want to sell items you buy at auctions. As you become familiar with your

---

$$ MONEYMAKER $$

Larry knew a lot about cars and their prices—both new and used. He decided to profit from this knowledge by trading one item of value for something of equal value, while building in an advantage for himself. He bid $25,000 for a Rolls-Royce at a customs auction. Three weeks later he traded the Rolls for a piece of real estate worth $50,000—the market value of the car.

---

field, you'll be able to develop marketing plans and find your own target clientele.

Don't let your auction career be cut short because you don't have enough ready cash to begin. Why not form a partnership with one or more people who have cash to invest? Plenty of people are interested in the profits that can be made at auctions, but they lack both the skills to buy intelligently and the time to invest in acquiring those skills.

Your knowledge of the field can provide benefits for them, because you're much more likely to make intelligent and informed auction purchases than they might. Your special expertise gives you the leverage you need to negotiate a mutually profitable partnership with other potential investors. You profit by having more cash to buy items; your partners profit because you're more likely to make intelligent choices at the auction and the subsequent resale. Everybody benefits.

CHAPTER **4**

Selling to Generate Profitable Cash Flows

Saving money on your personal purchases will improve your cash flow position, of course. But real profits come from using auctions and government sales to buy items you can resell to others for more than you paid yet at lower prices than the same items would cost your customers if bought at market value. The trick lies in knowing how to dispose of the merchandise once you acquire it.

When you're starting out small, with little cash to invest, you might specialize in clothing, small appliances and pieces of furniture, costume jewelry, novelties, records, musical instruments, or a variety of small goods. These are ideal for yard sales or flea market stalls.

For larger items, you can run classified ads in your newspaper. Whenever you get a good buy on a refrigerator, washing machine, car, motorcycle, large piece of furniture, or whatever, simply run an ad with your phone number. You can set a price or advertise it for "best offer."

Check out discount and secondhand stores as outlets for your purchases. When you can buy at very low prices in large lots, like the man who purchased all those desks for the office equipment store, these can be good outlets for you. Remember, though, that stores have to pay you less than they charge their own customers for the same merchandise. If you only have one or two pieces, you might be better off selling them yourself.

Let others know what you're doing. Often, people who don't go to auctions themselves wouldn't mind picking up the kinds of great buys you'll be getting. If you can find something they'd like at a low price and sell it to them for less than they'd have to pay in a store, they'll understand if you add in a little profit for yourself. Talk to friends, neighbors, business associates, and people you meet at church and social groups.

When you get a chance, make friends with people who buy at auctions. Walk up to them after the sale, while they're looking over their purchases, compliment them on the great bargains they got, and then ask, "What are you going to do with this stuff?"

That can be a real eye-opener. You'd be surprised at the number of people who quietly direct little discount sales clubs, or sell merchandise out of a room in their homes (check local zoning and business regulations before you try this), or keep a running ad in the local paper. Some of them even have stores and buy merchandise at auction more cheaply than they can order it from regular suppliers.

In fact, my accountant recently told me an interesting story about a pair of merchants who showed up regularly at customs auctions in Hawaii. It seems these two men owned a clothing store

---

$$ MONEYMAKER $$

Adrian's record collection was a sore point in his marriage—old seventy-eights and forty-fives that his wife constantly nagged him to throw out because they took up so much room in their tiny apartment. Adrian mentioned the problem to a friend at work, who asked if the collection included any 1950s records.

"Sure," Adrian replied.

"Can I borrow them to play at my high school reunion?" the friend asked.

"No, but I'll rent them to you," Adrian joked.

"How much?" asked the friend.

And that was the start of Memory Lane Music. Both Adrian and his wife now spend weekends spinning records for reunions, anniversaries, and theme parties or scouring yard sales, auctions, and used-record stores to add to their collection. They recently moved from the crowded apartment to their first house—one that includes plenty of storage for the records that helped them get there.

---

in Honolulu. They used to order dresses for their store from a factory in Taiwan. When the dresses reached Hawaii, the merchants would be contacted to pay the customs duty—which they always refused to do. Instead, they'd wait until the regular customs auction, then go down and bid on the dresses and get them for much less than the customs duty would have been.

This worked very well for them, until a competitor started showing up at the auctions and outbidding them. He paid more than the customs duty would have been but still less than the price the original two men had paid to the factory in Taiwan when they ordered the dresses.

You'll become familiar with people who work these or similar schemes as you spend more time at auctions. Watch the bidders. You'll soon get a feel for which of them are serious business people and which merely hobbyists, people who go to an occasional auction looking for bargains for their personal use.

LEARN FROM THE PROS

Once you've attended enough auctions, you'll realize that "professional" auction shoppers, bidders who treat auctions as a business, generally specialize in certain categories. Within those categories they may bid on every item, but when they aren't successful they always drop out of the bidding at some point. That point is usually the price they've determined allows them to resell the merchandise at the profit they need. If they can't buy at or below that price, they won't buy.

Take a lesson from these people. They're experienced and realistic about what it takes to profit from auctions. Follow their bidding example. Get to know them and find out what they do with the lots they buy.

As you gather information on where you can dispose of your auction purchases, you'll also start getting a feel for the kinds of prices you can charge. On small merchandise, note what similar things sell for at the outlets you'll be using for them. For larger items, watch ads in places you might try to sell through.

As an example, if you think you might be able to buy an airplane at a good price, check in the private pilots' lounge at your local airport to see what prices are advertised on their bulletin board. Talk to some of the pilots and find out what they'd pay for a plane; ask if they know someone who's in the market. Look through some magazines published for people who fly, and talk to local aircraft salespeople. And of course, if you've found what you think is a good buy, it would be worth paying an airplane mechanic to take an hour or so of his time to check it out. In the same way, if you were going to buy a boat, you'd talk to the people at the nearest yacht or boating club, read the ads in some boaters' magazines, and consult boat salespeople.

Find out what the going prices are for this kind of merchandise, how strong the demand is, and about how long it might take to find a buyer and close a sale. Learn if there are particular sections of the country where certain models sell well or types of people who are more likely to purchase. For instance, small aircraft and boats are popular with doctors, dentists, and other well-paid professionals, so if you bought one of these, you'd probably want to advertise in professional publications aimed at these groups.

The more you learn about auctions, and how to resell the purchases you make at them, the more opportunities you'll find. But the real key to success in this area is to specialize in certain types of merchandise. Immerse yourself in the subject and learn your market thoroughly. Since you can concentrate all your efforts in one area, you will find that *you* are quickly becoming the expert.

Another benefit of specialization is that you can become known as the person to ask when your customers brag about the bargains you sold them. This word-of-mouth advertising can bring you many

---

$$ MONEYMAKER $$

Lillian enjoys auctions as a hobby and particularly likes antique jewelry. She became so good at bidding for it that a specialty store made her their buyer on commission. The store pays Lillian's expenses to visit auctions within a three-state area and gives her a cash drawing account to buy with. When the store sells her purchases, Lillian receives 15 percent of the profit. In 1988 Lillian averaged $5,000 a month working weekends.

---

inquiries from others who would like you to look for similar bargains for them.

You could even find yourself in the same position as my friend Don. He started going to auctions simply because he wanted to save money on purchases for his family. He did so well that soon friends were asking him to pick up bargains for them, too. Then Don realized there were probably a lot more people who would like to buy the kinds of articles he was finding at auctions.

He started buying large lots containing several hundred items. Typical buys were gross lots of baseballs and golf balls, backpacks, and athletic socks. Whenever Don made purchases like these, he'd put together a little flier and mail it to groups he thought would be interested: community baseball leagues for the baseballs, country clubs and driving ranges for the golf balls, hiking clubs for the backpacks. (He included the athletic socks in every flier.)

From this small beginning, working nights and weekends, Don built his little mail-order business into a national sales catalog. He became well known to certain large manufacturers as a man who buys sports-related merchandise the company can't dispose of through normal sales channels. Now, when these companies are faced with inventory they can't sell, they often call Don and ask him to take it off their hands. Don decides whether he can sell it, and at what price, and then makes them an offer that provides him with a profit.

Sometimes, too, if Don doesn't think the merchandise is suitable for his catalog but knows someone else in his network of contacts who could profit from it, he'll act as a broker, or middleman, to put the right buyer and seller together. He takes a commission on these transactions. Result: the company cuts its losses, someone who can profit from it gets needed merchandise, and Don collects a nice fee for his knowledge and time.

That all came later, of course; but it started with auctions and knowing how to profit from them.

PLAN AHEAD

As you become familiar with the prices you can pay for auction merchandise and the ways to resell it, be alert to charges that will

---
$$ MONEYMAKER $$

George and Faye found their retirement income didn't stretch to permit the kinds of nice gifts they wanted to give their grandchildren. Then they started attending auctions and finding bargains in children's clothes and toys. They showed their good buys to their friends, and soon other older people who lived in their apartment complex started asking George and Faye to shop for them, too.

When the couple made good buys on gifts for their friends' grandchildren, almost everyone insisted on giving them a few dollars extra for their time and trouble. The local paper published a feature article about George and Faye, and these days the additional money they take in from their "shopping trips" covers the cost of everything they buy for their own family and helps them buy a few luxuries for themselves as well.

---

affect your final profit. If you plan to do any advertising, find out what the charges are for that kind of ad. Are you going to run a flea market stall? Learn what space rents for, and ask if you can get a discount by reserving for several weekends at once.

You might want to rent store space and run your own discount outlet. Figure up the charges for rent, insurance, business license, taxes, and any other costs of doing business in your city. Don't forget you'll need a sign, and you'll probably want to do some advertising. Decide whether you want to hire anyone to help you keep the store open; in addition to wages, you'll have to pay Social Security contributions, state disability and unemployment contributions, and the employer's share of any benefit programs.

For those who want to issue fliers, don't overlook the costs of doing business this way. You'll have to pay to get your fliers printed, and if you want something fancy, typesetting and artwork will add to your costs. (Many computers run graphics programs now; if you already have a computer and are interested in learning the programs, this can substantially cut the costs of producing your fliers.)

Then there's distribution: Are you going to put these fliers on windshields in the supermarket parking lot, hire someone else to do this, or send them through the mail? When you use the mails, you may have to rent mailing lists—look in your phone book Yellow

Pages under ''Direct Mail'' for companies that rent lists—and you'll certainly have to pay postage (ask at the post office about low third-class rates). If you're going to fill orders through the mail as well, you'll need containers to send the merchandise in, labels, tape, and again, postage.

Once you have a fair idea what your overall costs will be, you'll be able to make judgments about the price you can pay for items and still make a profit. My advice is to keep your overhead as low as possible, unless your actual long-term goal is to own a store or go into the mail-order business. My own preferred technique is to start out very small, with minimum costs. This might mean yard sales, flea markets, or running low-cost ads in local newspapers or ''shoppers,'' those little giveaway papers that are almost all ads.

As you move up to higher-priced items and build a network of contacts, you can concentrate on some of the luxury goods, advertising in outlets that appeal to the buyers of your special bargains. Like Don, you might do some brokering or even specialize in finding bargains for others, for a fee. Never lose sight of your final goal, whatever it may be; but if it's becoming as wealthy as possible in the shortest possible time, don't get bogged down in running a business that isn't your dream job. Instead, use all these opportunities as tools to generate the capital that will take you on to the next step, where you can find larger opportunities to generate even more capital.

Finally, here are two points you need to be aware of when estimating profits and planning what you can sell after an auction purchase:

1. **Auction terms or conditions may change right up to the time the sale starts.** Don't think that just because you attended several previous auctions and the preview for this one, you know all about how a sale is being run. Always check for bulletin board notices or handouts when you come in, so you won't be surprised by unexpected changes.
2. **Many auctions place restrictions on the sale of liquor.** These vary from place to place, but in general you can only buy liquor for your own personal use, unless you happen to

be in the liquor business and have the correct licenses and permits. If you do have the necessary paperwork to resell liquor, you must show it. In addition, you'll probably be required to pay state and local taxes on your purchase, which won't be included in the auction price. And, of course, you must be of legal age to purchase liquor.

As you learn your way around the auction circuit, you'll probably hear about more small local auctions held by private companies or individuals. That's great. Just remember that the rules may not always be quite the same; check them out before you bid.

Small or private auctions may not hold a preview before the sale and may not supply you with a catalog. In that case prepare yourself by arriving early enough to inspect the merchandise before the bidding starts. Carry a small notebook with you and write down the lots you're interested in and the maximum you'll bid for each. If there's no chance at all to view items before they go on sale, you should know your market well enough to be able to make fast decisions on how much to bid.

FINDING WHERE TO BUY

Now, how do you find out when and where the auctions are, so that you can start learning how to use them and get in on this bargain bonanza? For some types of auctions, the information is as close as your daily paper. Many, many auctions are advertised in newspapers. There's usually a section back near the classified ads where public notices are published, and you'll often find auction notices there, too. Another source for finding out about auction sales is your local legal publication. This is a newspaper that publishes all the notices of legal proceedings filed in your community. If you don't know the name of this paper, look in your Yellow Pages under "Newspapers" or ask your local bar association, a librarian, an attorney, or someone who works for an attorney. When you read these papers, you'll find out about many government auctions.

There are also special mailing lists you can get on for particular types of auctions. In fact, you should make an effort to get on as many lists as you can. Even if you're not interested in the types of merchandise they offer, or you can't afford to bid on higher-priced items just yet, you should start getting acquainted with these sources. The day may come when you'll want this information. It's free or available for the cost of a stamped, preaddressed envelope, so you might as well sign up for it before you become preoccupied with other matters and forget whom to contact.

There are enough auction information sources to fill an entire directory. I know that for a fact, because I've compiled such a directory, and it's more than 230 pages long. (I've provided the most important information sources at the end of this book.) But whatever source you use, I guarantee that there are many auction opportunities out there, just waiting for you.

CHAPTER 5

Local Profit Opportunities

As our first step into the world of auctions, let's take a look at some sales you're likely to find in just about any town of any size in the country. We'll talk a little about how the property reaches these auctions and the kinds of merchandise you're likely to find, and then we'll describe how to learn when and where these sales are held in your area.

POLICE AUCTIONS

Police departments frequently end up with items that no one claims. Most often these are items that have been found, abandoned vehicles, or items recovered in the course of an investigation and presumed to be stolen. If, after a reasonable length of time, no owner can be found—or in the case of towed vehicles, if the owner won't redeem the property—the police hold a public auction.

There's no telling what will show up at a police auction. You can get a pretty good idea of some likely items, though, by thinking about the sorts of things that are easily stolen and are hard to trace—cameras, car stereos, TVs, small appliances, coins, sports equipment, personal effects, and bicycles. In fact, police auctions are one of the best sources in the country for low-cost bicycles. Abandoned vehicles can be anything from a moped to a recreational vehicle.

Police auctions are advertised in the local newspapers. You can also get information about future sales by telephoning local police departments and getting on their auction mailing lists. Auctions usually come under the authority of the General Property Division, in police departments large enough to have one.

How often a police department holds an auction depends on how large the department is and how much property it accumulates. Even small-town departments usually have auctions once a year, while in larger cities there may be one every month or every week. As with private auctions, you'll have a chance to see the merchandise in advance before making your bids.

Items must be removed when the sale is over, although in the case of motor vehicles most departments allow you two or three days' leeway, especially if the vehicle has to be towed. If you don't remove your purchase within the time limit, the police or storage lot can charge you storage fees until you do; if you wait too long—generally longer than fifteen days—they have the authority to regard the property as abandoned and dispose of it as they see fit.

BANKRUPTCY SALES

Recently America has experienced a number of business and personal financial crises unequaled since the Great Depression of the 1930s, and I predict this situation will become worse in the 1990s. However, remedies are available to those who stand to lose everything when overstretched budgets reach the breaking point. Whenever corporations or individuals become insolvent, they can file a

---

$$ MONEYMAKER $$

Derek is only fifteen, but he's already learned how to profit from auctions. He attends four police auctions a year and buys all the bicycles he can get for 20 percent or less of their value. He repairs any damage, paints, and replaces missing parts, then sells the bikes to school friends. Derek estimates that he can buy and repair a bike worth $200 for an average of $60, then sell it for about $120. He's made $2,500 this way each of the last three years, and now he plans to move up to restoring old cars for larger profits.

---

petition for bankruptcy and stop creditors from attaching their assets. The purpose of bankruptcy proceedings is to convert the debtor's assets into dollars for distribution among the creditors. Personal bankruptcies have increased steadily in the past few years; the rate for 1988 was 60 percent higher than that for 1980.

To begin bankruptcy proceedings, an individual or corporation files a petition at their local bankruptcy court or district court if there's no specific bankruptcy court in their area. All liquidation proceedings are governed by the Federal Bankruptcy Act and subsequent amendments.

The bankruptcy court appoints a trustee in bankruptcy, who disposes of the debtor's assets subject to the court's control and direction. With the exception of certain personal property, any and all assets of the debtor's estate can be sold. (However, certain assets related to the debtor's ordinary course of business normally won't be sold; for example, a plumber who declared bankruptcy would be allowed to keep the tools needed to continue working and earning a living as a plumber.)

Assets can range from personal to real property, which means that in addition to real estate, individual bankruptcy sales often include furniture, jewelry, cars, tools, hobby and sports equipment, recreational vehicles, and boats. A business bankruptcy sale would include any assets used in the course of that business and available for sale (that is, not claimed for payments owed to whoever sold them to the business). Depending on the business, this could be almost anything: machinery and tools, office equipment, merchandise from a store inventory, and so on. If the business went under because management allowed itself too many luxuries—which is an all-too-common source of business problems—assets might even include such items as company cars, an executive plane or two, and maybe even some resort property.

Trustees in bankruptcy are private companies and, as such, make their own choices in the procedures they use to dispose of a debtor's estate. Generally sales are held at a public auction. The general public is notified and invited to bid. The trustees have complete jurisdiction over which auction house will handle the sale. In the case of real estate sales, some trustees will simply turn over

57

the property to a licensed real estate broker. If you happen to be a creditor, you will be notified at least ten days before any such sale is held.

The bidding procedures of a bankruptcy sale also vary, according to the individual trustee. Trustees can use both oral and sealed bidding to liquidate the assets. At oral auctions, competitive bids are accepted in typical auction fashion. At sealed bid auctions, the bidder simply writes down and "seals" in an envelope an offer for a particular item, usually along with a deposit of 10 percent of the amount of the bid in the form of certified funds. All of the envelopes are opened at one time, and the highest bid wins.

When the bidding is closed, the trustee must approve the bids and present the high bid to the court for confirmation. Usually the court will approve this bid, at which time the bidder must present full cash payment to the court.

Because of the specific rules involved in a bankruptcy procedure, bankruptcy sales usually take a few months to consummate. The time involved is commonly from thirty to ninety days and can sometimes take six months or more.

Your first important step in learning about bankruptcy sales is to get your name on the mailing list for your area. In some parts of the country, the bankruptcy court maintains its own mailing list for all auctions under its jurisdiction. In other areas, each trustee keeps his or her own list. Contact your nearest bankruptcy court for information on what system they use. (You'll usually find the bankruptcy court in the federal building in your area, and it should be listed in the "Government Offices" section of your local telephone directory. If you have difficulty finding it, ask the clerk at your county courthouse.)

—— $$ MONEYMAKER $$ ——

Sally couldn't afford to bid at bankruptcy auctions, so she hired herself out as a "finder" for other investors. She visits the bankruptcy court and goes through all the records, then notifies any of her clients of sales that might interest them. Whenever her clients make a successful bid on items Sally alerted them to, she receives either a finder's fee or a share in any eventual profits.

When you contact the bankruptcy court, ask to be put on its mailing list. If you live in a district where each trustee must be contacted separately, ask the court for the list of their names and addresses. In a few parts of the country, a United States trustee appoints the bankruptcy trustees and supplies the names and addresses. The court will tell you, and direct you how to contact the United States trustee, when this is the case.

Not only do you want to be contacted on the regular auction bid sales, but you want to keep in touch with the trustee for any negotiated sales. In these, the trustee finds a buyer who offers a price without going through competitive bidding. The trustee submits this bid to the court for confirmation and then gives the public an opportunity to overbid the offer.

When this happens, the court sets a minimum increase for all overbids. For instance, the court might require that all other bids must be at least $1,000 over the amount of the initial offer. If you think someone else might bid $1,000 over the existing bid, you could bid slightly more, such as $1,050, to give yourself a better chance of submitting a successful bid.

Certain auction houses specialize in bankruptcy sales, and they can be located in the Yellow Pages and by ads in local newspapers. Telephone them to get on their mailing lists as well.

As always, keep an eye on your local newspapers for advertisements of auctions and legal notices announcing bankruptcy sales. Remember that the legal requirement is only for a "newspaper of general circulation," so the advertising may be in a small paper, not the largest in the area, or may be in a legal newspaper, if there is one in your area.

UNITED STATES MARSHAL'S SALES

Here's a type of sale that used to be more of a gold mine than it currently is, but it can nevertheless turn a profit for a savvy buyer. U.S. marshals handle sales ordered by courts at the federal or local level. Sometimes they also wind up with property seized by the FBI for which the legal owners can't be found, property seized by the IRS, or anything else that might come under federal jurisdiction.

Although these items are usually turned over to private auction companies to be sold to the public, you can get an idea of what may be available for sale in the near future by looking for the legal notices.

Watch your local legal or regular newspaper for legal notices regarding marshal's sales or seizures of property. Although much of the property seized will be redeemed by the owners or creditors, and thus won't be up for sale, there is always property that's not claimed.

It can be worth your while to call your local U.S. marshal's office and ask them for the district National Asset Seized Forfeiture Program, which is in charge of disposing of the property. That office should be able to tell you what private auction companies they use. Then contact the auction companies to get on their mailing lists.

ESTATE SALES

There are really two different kinds of estate sales: those for personal property and those for real property (land, houses, apartment buildings, commercial property, and the like).

Real property sales are often handled as ordinary real estate sales, with an attorney or executor offering the property through a real estate broker. However, it's always possible for the real property in an estate to go to auction, especially if back taxes are owed on it. Sometimes, too, the attorney or executor will handle the sale of property personally, in an effort to save real estate commissions and obtain the most profits possible for the heirs.

Since real property auctions are covered extensively in a later chapter, our discussion here will concentrate mainly on personal property. This includes pretty much anything a person can own, from clothing and furniture through artwork and automobiles to machinery and farm equipment.

Property can come to an estate sale in several different ways. In the most clear-cut cases, a person dies leaving a will that states that the property is to be sold and the proceeds divided among the heirs. Or the will may simply leave the property directly to the heirs, who decide they have no use for it, or certain pieces of it, and determine to sell all or part of the inheritance.

In other cases, the person who dies may leave no will. If the heirs can't decide how to divide the property, they or a court may conclude that the best solution is to sell everything and divide whatever money the sale brings.

Still other cases involve those people who die without making a will and have no known heirs. In these circumstances the state receives the property. Since the state has no use for personal possessions, it holds an auction and claims the proceeds.

Settling a large estate can sometimes take several years. Complications following the death of multimillionaire Howard Hughes involved conflicting claims about various wills as well as the rights of former spouses, children, and more distant relatives, not to mention friends, business associates, and even casual acquaintances. When the stakes are high, as they were in the Hughes estate, even different states fight over which one should be considered the deceased's legal residence for purposes of claiming large inheritance taxes.

However, it's only when the property reaches the point of a possible sale that you really need to understand what's going on, although following the news of these valuable estates can teach you a lot. For instance, when an extremely rich and/or well-known person's estate is publicly fought over for a long time, you can assume all the publicity will draw a large crowd to any eventual sale. That's not the place to find the best bargains, since collectors and curiosity seekers will bid up the prices.

On the other hand, if the person was a celebrity or important figure, continuing fame may increase the value of his or her possessions. In that case, it could be wise to buy even at an inflated price, if you believe you can sell for an even higher price in the future.

If you want to try this, though, you need to develop judgment about whose reputation will continue to grow and whose will fade shortly after death. For instance, anything owned by international celebrities like Elvis Presley and John Lennon, or anyone historically important, such as a member of royalty or a former president, is likely to increase in value for years to come. But the demand for items once owned by a very minor celebrity is apt to be limited

61

to an extremely small number of people who are, therefore, unlikely to create a very rewarding market for that person's former belongings.

It may sound callous to talk about making a profit off the possessions of people who have died. What about the feelings of their families and the people who admired them in life? In fact, the personal property of a celebrity may be of little use to the heirs. Or it may have to be sold to pay taxes on the estate or to provide financial support for the heirs. And when you resell what you buy at a celebrity auction, you're creating an opportunity that might not otherwise exist for some serious admirer of that person.

How can that be? At auctions, items are normally sold in lots. A lot may be one item or it may be an entire box or barrel full of assorted objects. When a lot contains several articles, it may consist of only one or two really valuable pieces and a great deal of miscellaneous junk. Wealthy collectors often buy many, many lots and then keep the most interesting pieces for their private collections. The rest, which they see as having very little value, may be consigned to a specialty shop, sent to a seldom visited storeroom, or even discarded.

However, what the serious collector sees as junk may have sentimental value for a dedicated fan who can't afford to bid against the collector for the entire lot. But if you buy the lot, you can break it up into individual pieces for resale. The most valuable may still go to a wealthy collector. But less valuable pieces can be made available to the dedicated fans at prices they can afford.

Celebrity estate auctions, of course, are a special case, although they can be fun and profitable. But the same circumstances apply to estate auctions held for less well known people. When you buy at these, you know your cash is welcome to those who benefit from the sale. And when you find a willing buyer for your purchases, you've created a win-win situation, since you profit, and the person who buys from you has an opportunity to obtain something that might not be available from any other source.

There are three main ways to buy from estates. In the first, an executor publishes a notice in the general newspaper or the local legal paper. This notice states that items from the estate of a particular person will be offered for sale. The notice usually contains a request for people who are interested to contact the executor for further details and will give a name and address for that person.

If the sale includes real property, that fact will be mentioned, and the notice will usually state what the property is and where it's located. Terms of the sale and how to bid may also be included; for instance, the notice may say whether there is to be an open auction or if the executor is accepting sealed bids and the date and time when bids will be heard or opened.

The second method is to go to estate auctions held regularly by auctioneers. If you look in the Yellow Pages of your telephone directory under "Auctioneers," you'll find ads for companies that hold frequent sales of estate property. Some of them run notices that auctions are held regularly on certain days of the week or month; others will have to be called to find out when their sales are. Some will put you on their mailing list to receive regular notices of upcoming auctions.

You want to be careful when you attend auctions held by these organizations. Their sales often attract people who think that because it's an estate sale, everything will be sold cheaply. These people easily get caught up in auction fever and bid wildly, in many cases driving prices up far beyond an item's true value. If you realize an auction has drawn this sort of group, don't bother bidding against them.

The third method for buying from estates is to contact your local public administrator for listings of estate property. The public administrator heads a department usually associated with the county treasurer and/or tax assessor and deals mainly with real property. Sales run by these offices may be by either oral or sealed bid, depending on state regulations.

In a sealed bid auction, a deposit in certified funds must accompany the bid. This deposit is usually a percentage of the full bid, most commonly 10 percent. Bids have to be made on an official form, which is supplied by the office or individual running the sale.

You will be informed of deadlines for filing your bid and for presenting the full price (or proof of financing, where allowed) if your bid is successful.

After sealed bids are opened, some states allow the bidders to enter into oral bidding. Here again, you don't want to be stampeded into paying more than the property is actually worth to you.

Financing is generally the responsibility of the bidder. The administrator of the estate may refuse a bid, although this is rarely done, and the high bid must be approved by the court before the property is awarded.

STORAGE LOCKERS AND WAREHOUSES

Public storage auctions are a highly individualized type of auction; the procedures vary from place to place and from company to company, and the items offered for sale can include everything from personal property to heavy machinery. You've probably seen those businesses that supply small individual storage spaces people can rent by the month or year. Most of the ones I've seen look like rows of adjoining garages surrounded by a high fence. You can rent a storage space, or two or three, or however many you want, and use them to store whatever doesn't fit in your house. These businesses go by such names as Mini-Warehouse, Public Storage, Loc-n-Stor, and so on.

In addition, people have for many years stored unused goods in warehouses. Some of them belong to moving companies; others belong to companies in the storage business. People use warehouses for lots of different things. Often they move from a large house into a smaller one or into an apartment and store all their excess household goods and appliances. They may plan to move back into larger quarters eventually, or they can't decide to get rid of anything. Other users live in apartments to begin with and rent the storage space their homes lack. Sometimes roommates move in together, and one or the other stores extras and duplicates.

These people store things like living room and dining room sets, appliances from blenders and microwave ovens to refrigerators and dishwashers, clothes, paintings, lawn furniture, baby furniture, barbecue equipment, bedroom sets, china and silver, sports equipment such as surfboards and skis, board games and puzzles, children's toys, lamps, books, aquariums, TVs, stereos, records, bicycles, motorcycles—the list is endless. In brief, anything someone might own and keep at home can also be found in storage lockers and warehouses. Storage facilities with enough space also house dune buggies, RVs, boats, and trailers.

Other times, people have some sort of heavy equipment, usually connected with a business or hobby, which they can't keep in an apartment or small house. These people might store everything you need to work on cars, from wrenches and screw drivers to the lifts you use to take motors out of autos and the risers you use to raise the car high enough to work under it. I've talked to people who found well-drilling equipment and complete woodworking outfits, including band saws and lathes, in storage lockers.

People who plan to start a business, or who once had a business and think they might own one again, store items they believe will be useful. They can include large articles such as desks, file cabinets, computers, typewriters, and copy machines, as well as smaller supplies like pens, staplers, invoices, and receipt forms. Depending on the business, you might find heavy machinery, restaurant fittings and supplies, tools, hardware, or almost any equipment that can be used to run a store or service.

Active businesses also make use of public storage lockers from time to time. They might keep extra inventory in them or use them to warehouse some of their equipment. Sometimes these businesses stop operating or move away and forget or abandon the equipment in storage.

So you can see, there's really no telling what you might find at a public storage auction. These sales take place when the rent goes unpaid on the space for any length of time. Some warehousing businesses will act if the bill isn't paid for three months, some wait six months, and a few will go for an entire year. But at some point the management will open those lockers and sell whatever it finds to defray the cost of the unpaid charges.

Public storage auctions aren't organized in any one particular way, although none of the many I've investigated set any preview date or require you to preregister or pay a deposit. Instead, you show up on the day of the sale, and when the auction starts you bid either by signaling the auctioneer as he calls out numbers or by shouting out your bid.

Few of these auctions make any special effort to advertise publicly, and I've yet to run into one that keeps a mailing list. To find out about them, you have to keep an eye on the legal notices in your newspaper or the largest-circulation paper near where the auction will be held. These notices will give the time and date of the sale and list some of the merchandise to be offered (although these lists often include such descriptions as "75 cartons assorted household goods").

Some public storage facilities hold auctions once a month, while others go two to three months between sales. In most cases the management or owners simply reach a point where they decide, "Well, we're getting a little too much stuff taking up space around here," and initiate the legal steps that allow them to claim the stored items in lieu of rent.

Since these auctions are run by the people who own the storage facilities, the way goods are sold is the owner's choice. Sometimes a professional auctioneer is hired to take bids, but quite often the owner or manager is in charge. Bids may be taken on every individual item, or a lot may consist of all the contents of a locker. In that case you have to buy everything in the lot, even if you're only interested in one or two articles.

That shouldn't bother you if you're planning to make money from your auction purchases, however. After all, there's usually a way to sell almost anything you come up with. And remember, there are always those old standbys, the yard sale and flea market. If one person cared enough about something to store it, there's usually someone else who'd like to own it, too.

Purchases must usually be paid for in cash or certified funds at the time of the sale. Smaller facilities may accept local checks, but you'd better find out about this in advance. The sale notice will include the name of someone to contact about the auction and usually a phone number. In the case of storage businesses that are owned by a large company with a nonlocal phone number, you can

---

$$ MONEYMAKER $$

Sid doesn't bid at many auctions, but he visits many of them with a truck and a large supply of cash. When overenthusiastic bidders buy all-cash items and then come up short, Sid helps them make up the difference. He holds the item for thirty days for the bidder to redeem by paying back the loan plus a stiff interest charge. If they pay off their loans, Sid makes a tidy profit on the interest. If they don't repay their loans, he does even better, because they lose their purchases to Sid, who occasionally holds a sale of his own.

---

generally just call the local branch where the auction is scheduled for more information.

Local auctions are excellent places to pick up bargain merchandise on which to make your first profits. You can start small with items you can buy cheaply and resell quickly to increase your cash flow in a hurry. And, as you've seen, there are also opportunities to pick up some larger purchases—and make larger profits—as well.

CHAPTER **6**

Our National Bargain Basement

Opportunities for low-priced bargains probably exist at auctions right in your own hometown. But there is another group of auctions that may require a little travel for you to attend. They're sponsored by the federal government and are held not in every city, but in selected locations across the United States. The bargains they have to offer are well worth the travel time it takes you to get there.

U.S. POSTAL SERVICE AUCTIONS

Every year the various branches of the United States Postal Service end up literally with piles of items that they can't deliver and can't return. Sometimes the label has fallen off or can't be read; sometimes the addressee has moved and left no forwarding address, and the sender didn't include a return address. Occasionally someone refuses delivery on a parcel and for some reason it can't be returned.

Then there are goods that were broken or damaged in shipment, and the postal service has paid a claim but still has the merchandise. Not all of this is junk; some people won't accept anything that has the slightest scratch on it. Often the merchandise is still usable and could be sold to someone who is a little less particular. Sometimes, too, only part of the merchandise was damaged, but the addressee refused the entire shipment.

In addition, packages that aren't securely wrapped frequently lose some or all of their contents. The postal service employee who finds it can't know where it came from and thus labels it "loose in the mail." Anything that people ship through the mail—books, jewelry, stereos, video recorders, musical instruments, power tools, clothing, sports equipment, and cookware—can, for one reason or another, end up in a postal service warehouse.

Rather than let all these goods sit in a back room somewhere or throw them out, the postal service is authorized to auction them. Postal service auctions are handled by the main post office in each area and are held as often as necessary. For instance, the New York City area has a monthly auction, while the San Francisco area holds one four times a year.

All the post offices in an area ship their "dead parcels" to a warehouse under the supervision of the main post office for large combined sales. Most of these items go for amazingly low prices. The average video recorder at a postal service auction, for example, usually sells for somewhere between $75 and $100. Gold jewelry frequently brings 10 to 50 percent of its true market value.

Individual post offices also occasionally sell off equipment that has been used in the course of their business and is no longer needed. These sales may include desks, chairs, typewriters, file cabinets, and even motor vehicles.

Postal auctions are often advertised in the newspaper with the largest circulation in the area where the sale will be held. Fliers are posted on bulletin boards in main and local branches. If you call your nearest main branch and ask for information, someone there will be able to tell you when and where the next auction is being held or when one is due, if the notices haven't arrived yet.

You also may be able to get on a mailing list to receive fliers directly from the central post office in charge of auctions. In other areas you have to call the post office regularly to receive details of its sales. Check with your local main post office to find out what its policy is.

When you learn where and when the auction will be held, check for the time and place of advance viewing. As a smart bidder, you want to see what's available ahead of time if you can, so that you can decide whether you want to bid and how much money to bring with you.

The fliers list what items are scheduled for sale, but often these lists aren't precise. For instance, a notice I received for a San Francisco postal auction offered "books, jewelry, music recordings, stereos, and 725 lots of miscellaneous." When I arrived at the preview, I learned that "miscellaneous" included fur coats, golf equipment, lamps, blue jeans and shirts in a variety of sizes, hiking equipment, office supplies, baby clothes and car seats, balloons and party favors, electric guitars, framed pictures, porcelain figurines, and several hundred other real bargains.

Postal service auctions are run as typical oral auctions, but the details vary from one site to another. Some require you to preregister and pay a small refundable deposit of $20 or so for a paddle with a number that identifies you as a qualified bidder. At a few sales you can't get a paddle on the day of the auction but must pick it up during the preview. At these auctions no one is allowed to bid without a paddle. All sales are final, the goods are purchased "as is" and must be paid for in cash or certified funds at the end of the sale, and all purchases must be removed from the sale premises the day of the auction.

U.S. CUSTOMS AUCTIONS

Did you ever take a trip out of the country and come back through customs? If you did, you know that everyone passing through customs is asked, "Do you have anything to declare?"

$$ MONEYMAKER $$

Roxanne got her start with postal auctions. She would buy as much as she could afford of baby supplies, children's clothes, toys, small appliances, and miscellaneous housewares. Then every sunny Sunday she arrived at the local flea market early enough to get a good location at the end of an aisle and stocked her stall with all her postal bargains marked up to double what she paid. Her stall regularly brought in anywhere from $300 to $1,000 per weekend. Within two years she had the down payment on a home for her family.

What this question means, of course, is, "Are you bringing anything into the country that you are required to pay customs duty on?" Customs duty is a form of import tax charged on goods that people purchase in foreign countries and bring into the United States. If a traveler has something to declare, or if the customs agent searches his or her luggage and finds something on which duty should be paid, the traveler usually has two choices: pay the customs duty or have the goods confiscated.

More often than you might think, people either can't or won't pay the duty, and whatever they were bringing into the country is taken by the customs agent. After a waiting period, which allows travelers a little extra time to pay their customs duty, unclaimed items are sold off to the public at special customs auctions. Some of the most common items collected this way are jewelry, watches, clocks, liquor, and perfume.

That's only the beginning, though. Individual travelers aren't the only ones who abandon items at customs. All sorts of goods are shipped from all over the world to the United States, and for one reason or another, neither the sender nor the receiver will pay customs duty. Sometimes a business orders a shipment from a foreign supplier months in advance and then can't afford the duty when the shipment arrives. In other cases, an individual will send a friend a gift, but the recipient isn't interested in paying duty to claim the package.

As if that weren't enough, when someone is caught trying to smuggle illegal items, such as drugs, into the United States, it isn't just the illegal shipment that gets seized. Customs agents can impound any private vehicle that carries smuggled goods, too, and this can be sold at auction as well. In the way of cars this can be Porsches, Mercedes, and high-speed sports cars of all kinds. Smuggling generates huge sums of money, and the people involved in it regard fast autos as necessary business tools.

Then there are the smugglers' other favorite forms of transportation, sea and air. The number of boats and airplanes that end up on customs auctions is simply amazing. As an example, let me quote from an article that appeared in the *Houston Chronicle:*

Customs seizes an average of 15 to 20 boats a month, and there are usually 60 to 80 seized aircraft, some as big as DC-3s, stored at nearby Homestead Air Force Base. The confiscated boats and planes are sold to finance federal law enforcement activities.

An average of fifteen to twenty boats a month and sixty to eighty planes—and that's only for the area served by the Houston customs district. Plus just about anything that's manufactured in a foreign country can end up at a customs auction—and can be bought by you at auction for a fraction of what you'd pay retail! Remember the woman I mentioned in an earlier chapter who paid $15,000 at an auction for an airplane worth more than $100,000, then sold it for $90,000? She bought that plane at a customs auction.

Customs in every city with an international airport or border crossing collects something, every day of the year, and practically all of it goes up for auction. These sales are so exciting that when I sent a crew to film one of them, the director couldn't resist putting in a bid himself. He ended up buying a brand-new color television worth $700—but he paid only $130.

When a regional customs office seizes property, it files a Notice of Intent to Forfeit in the legal section of one or more local newspapers. If no one claims this property, the customs office turns over the sale and disposition of the property to its specialized customs broker, Northrop Worldwide Aircraft Services, Inc. (NWASI).

NWASI conducts sales throughout the continental United States, Puerto Rico, and Hawaii of forfeited seized property and general order merchandise for the U.S. Customs Service. These sales are conducted in the form of sealed bids, open bids, and public auctions. Items included in these sales are classified as vehicles, vessels, aircraft, real estate (both commercial and residential), general property, and general order merchandise. The general property or merchandise, in turn, can consist of a large variety of items such as gold, diamonds, emeralds, watches, miscellaneous wearing apparel in both commercial and domestic quantities, furniture, liquor, food products, high-tech equipment, electronics, machinery, and much, much more.

In fiscal year 1988, about two hundred customs sales were

73

conducted. NWASI holds regular scheduled sales every nine weeks in the following locations: Jersey City, New Jersey; Chicago, Illinois; San Juan, Puerto Rico; Los Angeles, California; Miami, Florida; Houston, Texas; Laredo, Texas; Nogales, Arizona; Edinburgh, Texas; Brownsville, Texas; and Del Rio, Texas. NWASI also conducts regular scheduled sales every six weeks in the following locations: El Paso, Texas; San Diego, California; Calexico, California; and Yuma, Arizona.

You can find out about these sales by watching the auctions section of your local newspaper or by getting in touch with NWASI yourself. NWASI provides information on their auctions through a one-year subscription program. Subscribers receive fliers or brochures on upcoming sales, descriptions of merchandise, specific terms governing each sale, and an automated voice mailbox and electronic message system providing the latest information on scheduled sales.

Subscriptions are currently available in three options:

1. **A nationwide service that includes the continental United States, Puerto Rico, and Hawaii.** The cost of this option is $50 a year for U.S. delivery and $60 a year for foreign delivery.
2. **A service for sales conducted in the eastern half of the United States and Puerto Rico.** The cost of this option is $25 a year for U.S. delivery and $35 a year for foreign delivery.
3. **A service for sales conducted in the western half of the United States and Hawaii.** The cost of this option is $25 a year for U.S. delivery and $35 a year for foreign delivery.

    To subscribe, send your name, complete mailing address, telephone number, and a postal money order for the option you select to

Northrop Worldwide Aircraft Services, Inc.
U.S. Customs Service Support Division
P.O. Box 2065
Lawton, Oklahoma 73502-2065

For more information, you can telephone NWASI at 1-405-357-9194 from 7:00 A.M. to 7:00 P.M. central daylight time.

GENERAL SERVICES ADMINISTRATION AUCTIONS

The United States government owns land, houses, and commercial and industrial property all over the country. This property was bought with our tax dollars, and now much of it stands empty. In some cases the branch of government that first acquired the property has outgrown the facility and moved somewhere else. Other facilities have been closed down or cut back in size and no longer need all the land and buildings they once used. And in some cases real estate was acquired in advance for a future project that never got off the ground.

Over the past few years, federal policy has encouraged the sale of much of this surplus and underutilized government property. The General Services Administration (GSA) is in charge of these sales.

Under GSA policy, when property is declared surplus, it is first offered to other federal agencies for their use. If no federal agencies can use the property, the next offer is made to public bodies such as state, county, and local governments. If no public body wants the land, it is then made available to the general public. Private individuals are encouraged to purchase these buildings and land and put them back into productive use. The government sees this program as a way to increase tax revenues and employment opportunities, so the GSA wants you to participate in its sales.

$$ MONEYMAKER $$

Scot specializes in electronic equipment at customs auctions—mainly VCRs, stereos and CD players, TVs, and cassette decks. Scot's friend runs a resort motel near the beach and allows Scot to display his auction purchases in the lobby. Vacationers can buy any of the equipment at discount prices or rent it by the day or week.

Scot says it's amazing how many people lose or break Walkman-type units on vacation and replace them; rainy days are good for VCR rentals. Scot's not telling how much this sideline earns him, but he recently cut back to half-time on his regular job so he could spend more time looking at investment property.

GSA auctions are sometimes also used as "catch-all" sales for other items the government owns and has no further use for. When offices close, unneeded equipment may go to the GSA to sell. Motor vehicles—cars, trucks, and jeeps—that have been acquired for government use or that have been confiscated from criminals by other branches of government, can end up at the GSA auctions. Occasionally, the GSA even winds up with boats once used by the U.S. Forestry Service. It's not always easy to predict what you'll find at some of these sales because the GSA is authorized to sell goods and equipment from so many sources.

Personally, I like to concentrate on GSA's real estate. There's such a variety, it's fun just to browse through its catalogs. If you think all that's apt to be available are some outdated government office buildings and a few abandoned airstrips, you're in for a surprise. Here are a few samples from recent GSA listings:

- A three-bedroom house on three acres of residential land in California
- A residence with more than an acre of land on the Gulf of Mexico
- An eighty-acre horse farm with two residences, five buildings, a pool, and a pond, in Florida
- A corner lot of one and a half acres across the street from a shopping center in Hawaii
- A 174,000-square-foot warehouse and 6.8 acres in an industrial park in Kansas
- Tracts of rural commercial/residential/agricultural land ranging in size from 20 to 120 acres in a national forest in Michigan
- Grazing land (120 acres) in New Mexico
- Forty buildings and miscellaneous structures, residential and commercial, on forty-eight acres in New York
- A golf course, 201.27 acres with five buildings, in Ohio
- An auto shop and a service station in Oregon
- Ninety-eight acres of unimproved industrial land near an airport in Texas

- Two 3-bedroom homes in Washington
- Eighty acres of timberland in Wisconsin
- Five 3-bedroom homes on five acres in Wyoming

That's only a sampling from one catalog. The point is, the GSA sells a wide variety of property all over the country, and they want you to buy it.

Most GSA properties are for sale by competitive bid, usually sealed, but sometimes at an oral auction. These sales are advertised in newspapers, magazines, and trade journals and on radio and television.

There's also a publication called the *Commerce Business Daily* that carries GSA auction notices and is available by subscription from

Superintendent of Documents
U.S. Government Printing Office
Washington, D.C. 20402

Prices change from time to time, so contact the office directly for the most recent information.

You can get a copy of the current U.S. Real Property Sales List, published every two months, by writing to

Properties
Consumer Information Center
Pueblo, Colorado 81009

When U.S. government real property is offered for sale, a local GSA real estate office prepares a notice briefly describing the property and explaining how, when, and where it will be sold. Notices are mailed to those who have indicated an interest in properties of that type, value, and location by writing to a GSA office. These offices are located around the country, as is shown in the list of addresses following.

77

U.S. General Services Administration Regional Offices

Region	Address	States in Region
1	John McCormick Post Office & Court House Boston, MA 02109	CT, ME, MA, NH, RI, VT
2	26 Federal Plaza New York, NY 10278	NJ, NY, Puerto Rico, Virgin Islands
3	9th & Market Streets Philadelphia, PA 19107	DE, MD, PA, VA, WV
4	75 Spring Street, SW Atlanta, GA 30303	AL, FL, GA, KY, MS, NC, SC, TN
5	230 S. Dearborn Street Chicago, IL 60604	IL, IN, MI, MI, OH, WI
6	1500 E. Bannister Road Kansas City, MO 64131	IA, KS, MO, NE
7	819 Taylor Street Fort Worth, TX 76102	AR, LA, NM, OK, TX
8	Building 41–Denver Federal Center Denver, CO 80225	CO, MT, ND, SD, UT, WY
9	525 Market Street San Francisco, CA 94105	AZ, CA, NV, HI, Guam, American Samoa, Northern Mariana Islands
10	GSA Center Auburn, WA 98002	AK, ID, OR, WA
National Capital	7th & D Streets, SW Washington, D.C. 20407	Washington, D.C., nearby MD and VA

When you see a notice for a GSA sale that you're interested in, you'll find a telephone number for the GSA regional real property office handling that sale on the notice. Contact the regional office and ask for an Invitation to Bid form. All sealed bids must be submitted on these forms. You'll receive all the instructions you'll need about time, date, and place of bids.

Usually the GSA does not set a suggested bidding price for its properties. It's up to the bidder to find out about the property values in the area and to come up with a reasonable assessment of what to bid. One way to do this is to check with real estate brokers in the area.

Sales are usually for all cash, although sometimes credit terms are offered by the GSA, depending upon its assessment of the marketability of the property. If the GSA thinks a property will be difficult to sell, it will consider offering credit terms. In any case, expect to include a deposit of 10 percent of your offering price with your bid.

The high bid has to be reviewed by the GSA, and if it is accepted, which is normally the case, an award is made within sixty days in most sales. The unsuccessful bidders receive their deposits back promptly. Should you be awarded the property, you will have an additional thirty days to pay the balance due.

You can, of course, buy anything at a government auction for your own personal use—and save a lot of money in the process. But most buyers have their eyes on bargains for quick resale—and quick profits. Why not become one of them?

PART II

Stepping into Wealth

CHAPTER **7**

Using Money to Make Money

The prices at both local and government auctions go far below what you'd find in discount stores or even from most wholesalers. Indeed, sometimes these are the prices the discounters and wholesalers receive when their merchandise goes for ten cents on the dollar in a bankruptcy sale.

If you never go any farther with the Cash Flow System than this, you already know how to save yourself hundreds or even thousands of dollars a year. It's no exaggeration to say you can save that much money when buying everything from appliances to cars, and even real estate, simply by bidding at an occasional auction. Those savings are dollars in your pocket to use as you see fit. Extra cash for the savings fund? A nice vacation? A better home? It's up to you.

My recommendation, though, would be to invest the money you save. Why invest it? To earn more money, of course.

Most of us don't learn much about investments during the part of our lives that's dedicated primarily to education. As I pointed out earlier, the main thrust of any education young people receive about money concentrates on getting a job. A course in economics might explain how the stock market works and how to shop for insurance, but that's about all the concrete information it contains. The rest is theory and general knowledge. Later on, after we've left school and have a job, we may hear about pension funds, money market funds, and so on, but whom do we turn to for complete explanations about these things?

Basically there are two sources of investment advice: brokers and the business media. Brokers, we know, want to sell us something. But did you ever ask yourself who sponsors the business media? Take a look at the ads in the magazines and newspapers, and even the television programs that give financial news. Who, for example, underwrites the public television financial discussions? Brokers, and companies and funds whose stock is traded through brokers, make up the bulk of the advertisers and supporters. Little wonder, then, that these programs and publications are aimed primarily at the person who already has large sums of money to invest, probably through a broker who earns a commission on every transaction. The other media that is addressed to the same audience are also represented among the advertisers, hoping for a share of the same pie.

But what about the average American who doesn't have a large amount of money to invest—or doesn't even understand the power of investments? Many of us say, "Oh, well, it takes money to make money," and resign ourselves to doing without.

It doesn't have to be that way. Once you understand a few key concepts, you can become financially independent and never have to rely on a job again. The first thing you must know is that building wealth does not depend on working for someone else and trying to save something out of the salary the boss decides you deserve. No one gets ahead that way. At best you'll end up with a small nest egg to supplement an inadequate pension.

YOU MUST TAKE CONTROL

The real cornerstone of any plan for financial success is learning how to multiply your assets. This means first accumulating a few assets and then putting them to work for you. Once you have some money or equity to put into investments, those assets will earn profits. As your assets grow, you use them to acquire more investments. This sets up a spiral effect. The more you invest, the greater your investment earnings are. The more investment profits you earn, the more you can invest, which again increases your profits.

Once you have a solid foundation of investments, you simply sit back and direct their growth. You no longer need to report to a job every day. You follow no one's schedule but your own. Your income doesn't depend on your turning out eighty-seven widgets that day, or being prepared at dawn for a power breakfast, or talking for six hours to a room full of people who would rather throw spitwads at each other than listen to you. If you don't report to the factory, office, or school, your money still rolls in, and no one puts a black mark on your attendance record. Your life is under your own control.

Sounds good, doesn't it? That's what I thought, in the years before I actually reached that point. Now that I've been there a while, let me tell you something. It *is* good! I wouldn't trade places with anyone.

Naturally you're more interested in your own financial security than in mine. You want to acquire those all-important first assets that get you started up the spiral of success, and I've told you how and where to do it—by buying at auctions. But remember, don't visit those auctions only to buy for your own household. Keep your eyes and ears open for ways to turn auction purchases into added income for yourself. Buy for friends, acquaintances, business contacts, and complete strangers who'll fill your pockets with dollars just for sharing with them a fraction of the savings available to you for knowing where and how to buy.

That's only the first step of your journey to financial independence, though. The next step of my Cash Flow System will take you all the way to your ultimate dream of wealth and financial independence.

CHAPTER **8**

The Fastest Route to Financial Independence

Some people are surprised to learn that real estate can be bought at bargain rates and with little or no cash outlay. Some believe it when they hear what others have done but never try it for themselves. Yes, they'll admit, they'd like to buy a home for themselves without making a big down payment; certainly they'd like to own some income property on favorable terms. But when it comes to doing something about it, far too many people become timid and hold themselves back.

Perhaps these people don't fully understand the opportunities that exist for them or lack the knowledge to take advantage of their opportunities. I assure you they exist. But first I'd like to outline why you should consider investing in real estate if you haven't already decided to do so.

True financial independence comes from having enough money, and enough control over your money, that you don't depend on anyone else for income or job security. In order to reach that point, it's necessary to find ways to multiply your cash flow quickly and by large amounts. When I put together my Cash Flow System, I studied all the ways I could find to multiply investments. I searched for an ideal place to put money and made up a checklist of all the benefits I'd prefer in my chosen investment. My list included the following:

1. **Low initial investment.** I wanted to be able to buy in with little or no capital to start.
2. **Good leverage.** I also wanted to use whatever cash I did invest as a lever to control something worth greater value. That eliminated many investments right from the beginning.
3. **Income.** Some investments only pay off when they mature or when you sell them. True, you could stagger your investments so that they pay off at regular intervals, or buy and sell as a continuing process; but I wanted to set up a system that generated income for both current expenses and continued investment with the least amount of supervision.
4. **Appreciation.** A good investment should also gain in value over time. With good management, the right investment should show both short- and long-term profits.
5. **Low risk.** Not being a gambler, I wanted to put my money where I had the best possible assurance of getting it back. Even if I made a mistake and didn't earn as much profit as I expected, I hoped at least to recover my initial stake.
6. **Liquidity.** As a precaution, I wanted to be able to release the bulk of my cash from my investment on short notice, with little or no delay, and without paying penalties for the use of my own money.
7. **Diversity.** The ability to place cash in several different markets would protect me; if one market didn't do well, others might do better. If the worst should happen on one investment and I lost every dollar I put into it, I wanted some alternate undertakings that could cover my loss and perhaps still allow me to show a profit.

With those seven criteria in mind, I made up an Investment Comparison Chart like the one below and used it to evaluate every investment vehicle I could think of. When a particular investment met one of my criteria, I gave it a plus; when it didn't match up to my ideal, I marked it as a minus. When I wasn't certain, I gave it a question mark.

For example, I could open a regular savings account with any

Investment Comparison Chart

	Low Initial Investment	Good Leverage	Income	Appreciation	Low Risk	Liquidity	Diversity
Savings	+	–	–	–	+	+	+
Stock Market	+	+	?	?	–	+	+
Commodities	+	+	?	?	–	–	+
Real Estate	+	+	+	+	+	+	+

amount of money I wished, small or large. Risk would be minimal, I could take my money out whenever I wanted, and I could diversify, in a manner of speaking, by opening accounts in many different banks, savings and loans, and so on. However, there would be no leverage involved; I would control nothing of greater value than the dollars I personally deposited. Income from the interest I earned would be low, and once I paid income tax on the interest and inflation ate away at the rest, my earnings would amount to almost nothing. Rather than appreciating, the money I saved might even lose relative value the longer it stayed in the bank.

HOW SAVINGS ACCOUNTS CAN LOSE IN VALUE

Could that be true? Let's see. Say I deposited $100 in a savings account at 6 percent interest for one year. During the year, then, my account would earn $6 in interest. If my tax rate on that interest were only 15 percent, I'd pay 90 cents to the government, bringing my earnings down to $5.10.

At the same time, let's say inflation during that year amounted to 4 percent—a reasonable figure, going by the rates of the past few years. That means that at the end of the year, my money is worth 4 percent less than it was when I deposited it, or $96. Of course, my $5.10 worth of interest is also worth 4 percent less than it would have been a year ago, too; it's actually only worth $4.82. On paper, I have $105.10, but my real buying power, compared with when I started, is $101.32. Not much progress, is it? And if inflation rose only a little, even that small gain would disappear. I could very easily be put into a position where I lost money by putting it into savings.

Obviously, then, in order to increase my initial investment, I needed ways to increase my money by larger amounts with higher rates of return. Extremely high risk propositions, such as oil wells and race horses, make no sense when you want safe investments. Stocks and commodities offer good leverage when you buy on margin, and there's certainly plenty of diversity, but the income and appreciation are highly unpredictable.

THE FASTEST ROUTE TO FINANCIAL INDEPENDENCE

HOW REAL ESTATE COMPARES

Finally I came to real estate and found it offered everything I was looking for. It's possible to buy property with very small initial outlays and even with no cash at all. The leverage is great, since it's customary to control real estate with an initial payment of only a fraction of the property's worth. Before ever buying a property, I could make extremely close estimates of its future income.

As for appreciation, historically the price trend for real estate in this country has risen steadily. During certain economic cycles in particular parts of the country, prices remain stable or drop, but eventually values start upward again. Depending on my plans, I could deliberately buy in areas with depressed markets and hold real estate until it gained value, or avoid those markets in favor of regions where prices were climbing steadily.

Once I began to understand real estate, I realized how little risk this investment holds. You do have to understand the market and know how to buy correctly, but once you do, it contains less risk than any comparable venture. Real estate is no one market, following the same trends throughout the country or even all over the world. Instead, every town contains some neighborhoods where prospects are better than in others. Some towns and even states are more profitable than others. The major principle involved is to become familiar with various markets and know how to buy in each one. Once you learn that, your risk is minimal.

Liquidity? You can sell most property fast by reducing the price below market value. If you've bought right, you'll still make a profit. When you don't want to sell, you can borrow against the property, either by taking out a new loan against it or by creating your own note, then using the note as cash (we'll discuss this more in chapter 16).

As for diversity, I've already mentioned the many different markets that exist for real estate. Within each of these markets, there are dozens of different kinds of properties, each with its own individual prospects and advantages.

With all these pluses going for it, I set out to learn more about real estate. It didn't surprise me when I discovered how many people

---

——— $$ MONEYMAKER $$ ———

Given a choice between going directly to college after high school or getting started in a home of his own, Tod asked his folks to buy him a house. Rather than a single-family home, though, he asked them to buy him a run-down duplex with a detached cottage in the backyard. Tod lived in the cottage and rented out the duplex units while he fixed up the property. After a few months he sold the duplex for a profit, negotiating to stay in the cottage rent free for two years, and bought himself two more run-down duplexes.

A year later Tod had those two in good repair, sold them, and bought a small apartment house. After some repairs he sold that and bought a slightly larger apartment building. With a steady flow of income, he enrolled in college while continuing to parlay his properties into larger and larger figures. As a result Tod got his bachelor's degree and still became a millionaire before age thirty.

---

had come to the same conclusions I did. Some of the largest and oldest fortunes in the world are invested in real estate; when Arab sheikhs strike oil, they buy property. The Rothschilds, the Rockefellers, and the queen of England own land and buildings all over the world. Obviously I was in good company.

WHERE TO START

Once real estate became the clear choice for my ideal investment vehicle, the next question arose: Considering all the different types of property available, where would be the best place to start?

Being a young man in a hurry, I didn't want to start with something that would take years of study to understand and then more years to start realizing profits. In a short time I narrowed down the field to single-family homes, for several reasons.

1. **Homes are affordable.** Contrary to what many people say these days, it is possible to buy homes cheaply, often with little or no cash outlay. Later we'll cover several ways of doing that. In addition, of all types of developed real estate, homes are generally the lowest-priced. True, you

can often buy raw land for less. However, land brings in no income to defray costs of ownership and calls for specialized knowledge if you want to make consistently high profits.

2. **Homes are easy to understand.** We all have some idea of whether a neighborhood is good or bad, how attractive a home is, and whether it's in good repair. And the one area in which you can become an expert most easily is your own and surrounding neighborhoods.

3. **Homes are easiest to buy.** The main considerations in buying a home are whether the buyer and seller can agree on price and terms. You don't have to get involved in construction permits, zoning requirements, environmental impact statements, market studies, traffic flow and parking considerations, or any of the other factors related to buying most other kinds of real estate.

4. **Homes are readily available.** You can find single-family homes in every part of the country, in every market, and in a wide range of prices. Sometimes you have to invest in an area outside your immediate neighborhood to find the price you want to pay, but the right properties do exist.

5. **Homes are in demand.** People always need places to live. We've heard a great deal of talk in the last few years about how difficult it is for the average family to buy a home. If these people all knew and used the techniques of the Cash Flow System, they wouldn't have that problem; however, many either don't learn or are reluctant to try creative buying procedures. As a result, over 40 percent of the population rent living quarters, even though the overwhelming majority of them would prefer to live in single-family homes. When you own a home you have a built-in rental market, and when you decide to sell you can often help a tenant become a homeowner by structuring the deal in such a way that you both profit. (We'll discuss ideas for doing this in chapter 15.)

Those are the main reasons for specializing in single-family homes. Naturally one of the first things you can do with my Cash

Flow System is use it to buy a home for yourself. Many of my students have done this and then go no farther. That was their main motivation for learning the system, and if they're satisfied, I'm happy for them. However, those of you who want to reach beyond mere satisfaction to total financial independence will want to learn how to buy an investment property rather than just a home.

CHAPTER **9**

The Difference Between a House as a Home and as an Investment

The number-one difference between buying a home and purchasing an investment house is the buyer's motive. An investment's sole purpose is, or should be, to earn money. This means you buy only for sound financial reasons. Emotional factors have no place in your decision to buy investment real estate.

When you look at investment property, therefore, you use different guidelines from those you use when shopping for your own home. Never mind the breathtaking view, or the cheerful yellow kitchen, or the fact that you hate green siding with white shutters. You're looking for a house that will appeal to a solid pool of renters or buyers and that you can rent and/or resell at a profit, according to your own plans.

This brings us back to your plans. Remember the equation I spoke of earlier? *Plan + Discipline = Success*. You have to keep that in mind as you decide what course to take with real estate investments. Some people prefer to buy property, install tenants, and hold for a few years of steady income before they sell. Others like to buy at bargain prices, then sell within a few months for large, fast gains. Still others combine these techniques, holding some properties and reselling others, for a combination of benefits.

When you decide to buy any property, you should choose which technique you plan to try before you make a purchase offer. You may wish to shop with both ideas in mind, weighing whether each property you see might be better used for continued income or a quick profit. However, before you sign any papers, be sure you know which course to pursue for that particular property.

WHICH PROPERTIES ARE MOST PROFITABLE?

Real estate has thousands of different markets, each slightly different. You must become acquainted with conditions in your own market area and learn to make your own judgments. But I can give you some broad guidelines to follow. In general, two kinds of single-family properties offer the best investment opportunities: the rental home in a solid, established neighborhood and the fixer-upper.

Buying to Rent

Look for rental homes in middle-income neighborhoods where more than half of the residents own their own homes. Only a few years ago all of the people already living in these neighborhoods would be middle-income workers with steady jobs. These days, however, you're also likely to find a sprinkling of young high-income professionals who haven't been working long enough to save the down payment they need to move into the more exclusive districts where their older colleagues live.

Most residents of good investment neighborhoods will be couples with children, although here again times have changed. Several single people sharing a house or two divorced parents combining forces to bring up their families together may be found in a few of these houses.

What you're looking for above all is a neighborhood where people have a sense of pride in their homes and are willing to settle in and raise children. Avoid high-crime areas and outright slums, where property values can decline rapidly. Look for neat yards, clean cars, and other signs of regular maintenance. A location with good access to transportation, shopping, desirable schools, parks, and other amenities is important.

96

Avoid the highest-priced, most luxurious neighborhoods of town. When you purchase for a high price, you have to charge high rents. Meanwhile, whenever the economy cycles into a downturn, people who have been living beyond their means cut back, and one of the ways they economize is by moving to a less expensive home. You'll have a more difficult time finding tenants for high-rent homes and more difficulty keeping them rented.

Besides that, even in the best of times the people who rent higher-priced homes usually make poor tenants. They pay top rents and expect the best service and can be extremely unreasonable in their demands on a landlord. When it comes time to sell, too, the house in the middle-income neighborhood appeals to the widest range of buyers, since fewer people can afford higher-priced homes.

Buying to Fix and Resell

Many people misunderstand fixer-upper houses, or "fixers." There seems to be a widespread idea that buying a house to fix it up automatically means becoming involved in months of tearing out walls, rebuilding ceilings, and letting yourself in for more work and aggravation than most people care to tackle. Happily for those of us who invest in real estate, this is simply not true. It can happen, if you don't buy correctly and don't consult an experienced building inspector or contractor, but such misadventures are unnecessary.

The average person looking for a house to buy does not understand the importance of minor cosmetic improvements. New carpet, a thorough cleaning, a fresh coat of paint, and a touch of yard work

---

$$ MONEYMAKER $$

Tina offered to buy a house at close to the market price, which she planned to resell for a quick profit. She asked that the deal include the kitchen appliances, washer and dryer, all the furniture, the gardening equipment and lawn furniture, and a large carton of spare machine parts in the garage. As the sellers said no to each request, they allowed Tina to reduce the purchase price with each refusal. By the time negotiations were done, Tina had managed to bargain the price down by $5,000 and was positioned for a clear profit at resale.

---

can add many times their value to the price of a house. Many of my students have proudly reported profits of anywhere from $10,000 to $70,000 on one house merely by making those minor improvements.

Here are good things to look for in a simple fixer. Shabby carpets or linoleum, scuffed or peeling paint, dirt and grime, and dead or unkempt lawns and shrubs are signs that you stand a good chance of buying below market value and profiting by many times more than the cost of improvements. However, before you make an offer on a house like this, or on any house you have any doubts about, do one of two things: either write up your offer as ''subject to inspection'' or hire an inspector to make a thorough evaluation of the property before you make an offer.

''Subject to inspection'' is one of the ''Houdini clauses,'' as they are called. These clauses allow you to escape from a deal if it turns bad on you. The inspector's report may turn up anything from crumbling foundations to a worn-out roof, and you don't want to buy into problems that would cost so much to repair that you couldn't make a profit.

Other points to watch out for are leaking foundations, dry rot, termites, kitchens and bathrooms that need complete remodeling, and bad plumbing, heating, and electrical systems. When you find your dream house and it has a few flaws, you may choose to buy it and fix it up. But as an investor who's interested in making maximum profits with minimum outlays of time and money, avoid these problems.

Here are a few other considerations you should keep in mind when buying any investment home:

- Corner lots on a direct route to a school or park tempt children to take short cuts across the lawn. Few people enjoy living with this traffic, and it causes damage. Avoid these.
- Most people enjoy peace and quiet at times, no matter how noisy they may be themselves. Don't buy on busy main streets or adjacent to public places or businesses that generate a lot of noise or traffic.
- Stay as far as possible from city dumps, sewer plants, refin-

eries, and similar facilities that generate unpleasant odors and, possibly, toxic waste. Given a choice, the majority of renters and buyers prefer fresh air.

LEARN YOUR MARKET

When you start to invest in real estate, you must learn how to judge whether or not you can make a profit on any property you look at. You need to know what constitutes a good price to pay, how much rent you can charge on income property, and what price you can expect to realize when you sell.

The best way to learn these facts is by learning about the market where you plan to invest. Start with the local newspaper's Sunday real estate section. Read the advertisements and learn the price ranges for new and resale properties and the going rents. Then go out and visit houses in person.

Don't simply look at the homes for sale. Inspect the homes for rent as well. This gives you firsthand knowledge of what rents are charged for particular kinds of homes. Check back later to learn how long it takes for the rentals you looked at to be filled. You can keep track of the ads and see how long they run or call the landlords at two-week intervals to see if the property is still vacant.

You may learn from this survey that your area is a "soft" rental market—that is, that rental houses stand vacant for long periods. You may also find that rents are low in comparison with the price of houses. If this happens, simply regard it as a small problem to be solved and consider alternatives. You might do better buying and reselling rather than buying to rent. Another neighborhood, possibly

---

$$ MONEYMAKER $$

Barbara and Phil bought the worst-looking house in a working-class residential neighborhood, but it was structurally sound and they got it for $15,000 less than neighboring houses sold for. Putting in time on evenings and weekends, they painted, recarpeted, put on new window shutters, and turned the house into a showplace. When they were finished, they had the nicest-looking house on the street and sold it for a $25,000 profit.

---

in a different town or even another state, might prove more profitable.

HOW MUCH IS THE PROFIT?

How can you tell whether a property will be profitable or not? Your market survey will give you much of the information you need. Then consider what has to be done. If you can buy a fixer for $10,000 under market value, how much will the repairs cost? How much will the house sell for after you've improved it? When you sell, will you pay an agent's commission of 6 to 7 percent of the sale price?

If you're planning to rent out the property for a while, you have a few other figures to deal with. You can't always assume that your rental will be snapped up the day you take possession and that the tenants will pay their rent promptly on the first of every month. Allow yourself a safety margin. Plan on two to four weeks of vacancy per house every year, and realize that while the house is vacant, you'll have expenses in addition to the regular payments. Cleaning and fresh paint may run between fifty and three hundred dollars for every vacancy. In addition, you'll have advertising costs when the property is ready to rent again.

Don't forget, too, that regular payments include more than just the mortgage or trust deed. You'll probably have to keep the utilities turned on to provide water for cleaning and lights for working or showing the rental at night, plus heat or air-conditioning, depending on the weather. If your insurance and taxes on the property aren't included in the monthly mortgage payment, you have to provide the money.

So add up the mortgage payments and other expenses, plus the cost of having the property vacant for a month out of the year. Then add up what rent you can charge for eleven months. Are the figures approximately the same? If the rent figure is significantly higher, you've got a sure winner. But when the expense total is higher, you need a way to make up the difference.

At this point some people become discouraged and decide they'll never be able to invest in real estate. They believe they have to come up with a down payment equal to 10 or 20 percent of the

100

property's value and then spend extra money to cover a negative cash flow.

That's not really true. When you buy correctly, you don't pay full price. You don't always have to come up with a down payment. You can lower the monthly payments to the point where you break even or profit, and you can increase the amount the tenants pay you.

When you deal in single-family homes, there is no limit to the flexible ways you can arrange price and financing to benefit you and help you achieve your financial goals. But first and foremost, there are several ways you can buy real estate at bargain prices.

CHAPTER 10

Make the Government Your Partner

The United States government sponsors a remarkable number of little-known programs designed to help people buy and repair real estate. The Department of Housing and Urban Development's guide, *Programs of HUD,* 1986/1987 edition (the most recent edition available as I write this), contains almost one hundred pages listing the bare outlines of these programs.

Some HUD programs provide information; some fight discrimination; but most help people find suitable places to live, whether through rent subsidies or mortgage insurance. The Veterans Administration (VA) and the Farmers Home Administration (FmHA) also sponsor favorable loan programs to enable people to buy and own real estate, build new structures, or rehabilitate run-down property.

By "favorable loan programs" I mean those with low down payments or no down payment at all, lower interest rates, and assumable mortgages. Many of these loans help first-time buyers get started in their own homes, whether it's a single-family house, a condominium, a cooperative, a duplex, or a small apartment house.

If your goal is to become wealthy starting from scratch, there are government loan programs to help you buy and fix up older homes and apartment buildings. If you're elderly or handicapped, federal programs will help provide you with affordable housing. Do you have credit problems? There are loans for people who don't qualify for conventional loans using bank lending standards. Are you a health professional who would like to own your own clinic or help your community improve its medical facilities? The government has programs for you.

Do you think home ownership is priced out of your reach forever? You'll find possibilities in foreclosures, manufactured homes, or the Farmers Home Administration program. On the other hand, if you're more interested in real estate investments, you'll find opportunities galore, whether you want to construct or just purchase. You might want to invest in a mobile home park, or a hospital, or an apartment house. For an apartment house the government will help you find tenants, subsidize your rents, and advise you on management. If you're a veteran or on active duty in the armed forces, there are special government loan programs just for you.

CHECK STATE AND LOCAL PROGRAMS

Besides the federal government, most states, and many counties and cities, have their own plans to help people buy, build, or repair property. For instance, many cities have redevelopment programs

---

———— $$ MONEYMAKER $$ ————

One worry that holds back people from investing in real estate is concern about having an empty rental unit with the mortgage payment coming due. That can be a potential problem, and one simple solution is to participate in the program known as Section 8 Guaranteed Housing for Landlords and Tenants, a government program designed basically for moderate- to low-income housing. The government will qualify your housing unit and the tenant, and guarantee your payment for a majority of the rent. The tenant will pay a small amount. Not only are you guaranteed the rent, but the government will also help you fix up the rental if it's left in a mess by a tenant. This rental program is one way Donald Trump's father built the real estate empire worth $250 million that Donald took over. It's a good program run by the FHA for large cities and low-income areas.

---

and offer loans or grants to encourage people to move into areas targeted for development or rehabilitation. States often have special loan programs to aid first-time buyers or residents who have trouble getting conventional loans.

The state and local programs are numerous and varied. You'll have to do your own research, but it isn't difficult. Simply look under the government listings in your telephone book for your local, county, or state Housing Authority or Housing and Community Development. The Housing Authority usually oversees rent subsidy programs for low-income and elderly people. Housing and Community Development oversees rehabilitation loan and bond programs. In some areas the two are combined, under the title of either Housing Authority or Housing and Community Development. It's not hard at all to find the information you need; it merely takes a few phone calls.

Why should you do this? These local government-sponsored programs usually offer excellent terms and incentives. For instance, at a time when the conventional loan rate was between 14 and 15 percent with a 20 percent down payment required, many cities were offering home loans at below 12 percent with only a 5 to 10 percent down payment. Reductions like that can make the difference for many people trying to qualify for real estate loans.

CONSIDER THIS A BEGINNING

Be sure to contact these government agencies yourself and get all the information you can directly from them. Your real estate agent or local lender may not tell you about these loan programs. In the first place, they may not know about them. Although they are familiar with the most common loans, they aren't likely to know all the available programs. Second, they may not be particularly interested in handling government loans.

You see, the government is committed to protecting you, the borrower, rather than to helping an agent or a loan officer make a quick commission. When you buy, build, or repair with a government loan, the property must meet certain standards. HUD, which is in charge of most of these loans, wants to be sure that you don't pay more than the fair price. If you need construction or repairs, HUD will go over your plans to be sure they are workable and that your suppliers or contractors deal fairly with you. All this involves a certain amount of paperwork, inspections, and meetings. The lender and the real estate agent have to fill out forms, answer questions, and steer your application through the government's approval process. This makes more work for them and takes a little longer than local bank approval.

That's why you should be familiar with the available government programs. You must know what you want and how to find it for yourself. After that, you'll need a real estate agent and a lender who will work with you. The place to start is the telephone directory. Often lenders will advertise that they have FHA or VA loans. Or your local HUD office (listed in your telephone directory under "U.S. Government") may have a list of HUD-approved lenders in your area.

HUD or the VA are ready to answer your questions. They can save you a great deal of time and many problems. For the most part these people are warm, friendly, and very helpful. They are full of information and are very willing to share it. Most government housing agencies also publish information pamphlets, which they're glad to send if you ask for them. Don't be reluctant to ask. Remember, these loans are for you, designed by your own government to make it easier for you to own real estate. Whether you want a mobile home, a single-family house, a rural home, a small apartment building, or a share in a cooperative or condominium; whether you want to buy, build, or fix up a property—there is a program for you.

FHA/HUD FORECLOSED PROPERTY SALES

The Federal Housing Administration (FHA) is an agency of HUD. Whichever name you call it, this agency is a national source of good property at discount prices. (Usually we speak of FHA loans and

FHA foreclosures, but if you hear someone speak of HUD fore-closures, it amounts to the same thing.)

There are dozens and dozens of FHA loan programs for buying, building, or rehabilitating property from mobile homes to apartment buildings. These loans are generally made directly to the borrower by banks or savings and loans and are guaranteed by HUD. If the borrower defaults and the lender forecloses on the property, HUD will pay the lender the balance of the loan and take ownership of the foreclosed real estate.

This is where it gets interesting for you and me. HUD is not set up to manage property and simply wants to resell it for a price that will cover its expenses. The expenses include the money used to pay the lender's loan costs and any maintenance or repairs done while the real estate is under HUD's ownership. If the mortgage is rela-tively new, the sale price of the property may be near its market value but most likely will be less. Although the sales are usually on an all-cash basis, some homes will qualify for FHA financing if they meet minimum HUD standards.

Most HUD property is sold on an as-is basis, which means it's the buyer's responsibility to take care of repairs and maintenance and to bring the property up to local codes. For this reason, be sure that someone familiar with construction inspects the property before you buy it. Obviously you don't want to buy any real estate that would cost so much to repair that there wouldn't be any profit left after you sold it.

If you're short on cash and can't find a partner, you might make some fast cash with these properties by becoming a "finder" for someone who specializes in rehabilitation work. You could locate or buy the properties and turn them over to the rehab worker for a fee or a share in the profits.

It's very simple to get a list of HUD foreclosed properties for sale. Simply call your local HUD office and ask for one. This office is usually located in the Federal Office Building nearest you. Since HUD sales procedures vary somewhat by locale, if you're interested in property outside your immediate area, check with your local HUD office to see which office has jurisdiction over that area.

—— $$ MONEYMAKER $$ ——

Four young women I'll call Lori, Rose, Kathy, and Teri met at their church singles' group. All four worked as secretaries or office managers and wanted to get ahead. Rose had a small inheritance of $5,000, Kathy had a $2,500 college fund she hadn't used, and Lori and Teri each had about $1,000 in the bank. They combined their savings, borrowed a bit more from their parents, and bought a run-down house in a decent neighborhood.

While it was structurally sound, the interior of the house was dirty, the carpets were stained, the wallpaper was torn, and painted walls bore finger marks and dirt streaks. Cupboards, closet doors, and woodwork had been scratched and gouged, and the linoleum in the kitchen and bathroom was cracked. Besides that, the front and back yards were bare dirt and contained low places that turned into mud wallows in wet weather.

The four friends paid $10,000 down on a $100,000 purchase price and financed $90,000 through an FHA loan. Each young woman paid $200 a month on their $800 payment—much less than each had paid as apartment rent. Working a few evenings and weekends and getting friends to help on the difficult parts, they painted and papered, refinished the cupboards and woodwork, installed new carpet, and landscaped the yard.

Three years later the property was worth $130,000. The four women sold it and used their profits to buy two 3-bedroom houses. Lori and Rose live in one, Kathy and Teri in the other, and each pair rents their extra bedroom to a boarder to help with the payments. In two or three years they plan to sell again and buy four houses—one for each of them.

You can also get on the national mailing list for multifamily project sales. To do this, send your name, address, and daytime telephone number to

HUD Multifamily Sales
Caller #10902
Alexandria, Virginia 22301-0902

or telephone 1-703-971-3618 with that information.

The foreclosed property listing is published weekly and includes the minimum price and bidding instructions as well as how to get any future lists you may need. The list should also come with instructions on how to bid; if it doesn't, inform the HUD office that you're interested in buying a property and want instructions. Bids are usually accepted for two weeks after a property is listed.

HUD requires all buyers to go through licensed real estate agents of the buyer's choice. HUD also maintains a list of real estate agents in each area, if you wish to use it. Any real estate agent in good standing can also help you in formulating your bid. The agent's fees will be paid by HUD.

Although HUD will provide a *suggested* price for a property, potential buyers are free to bid either above or below that price, if they wish. Most HUD sales are on a sealed-bid basis, with a deposit in the form of a cashier's check, certified check, or money order equal to 10 percent of your bid price. All sealed bids are opened at a specified time, and the highest acceptable bid generally buys the property. Unsuccessful bids and deposits are returned by certified mail.

HUD's definition of an acceptable bid includes the use to which the buyer intends to put the property and HUD's estimate of how suitable the buyer is for that property. For instance, if the property is a single-family home, an owner-occupant bid will get preference over an investor who wants to use the house as a rental. If it is a vacant lot, someone who owns adjacent property will be considered first.

The FHA is not obligated to accept bids below the asking price but has done so under certain market conditions. In 1988 a federal judge ruled that the FHA could not sell properties at auction for below the market value of similar properties in the area. The FHA has appealed, but at this time the outcome is uncertain. It will be necessary for you to check with the local HUD office to find out how the ruling is currently affecting the sale of foreclosed properties in your area.

You can, of course, offer more than the asking price, and you may have to. But remember, never pay any more than the property is *really* worth, and always know how you are going to make a profit. It means bidding low and maybe bidding on lots of different houses until one is finally accepted.

If there are no acceptable bids on a property on the date of the sealed bid opening, HUD will consider acceptable bids on a first-come, first-served basis. These are submitted on the same forms as sealed bids but are unsealed and can be submitted until the property is sold. Accepted bids have forty-five days to close. If a sale does not close in that time, HUD has the choice of accepting the second- or third-highest acceptable bid or of listing the property again.

Once you get the list of available properties, you should drive by any house that sounds promising. If you're interested, you'll need an authorized real estate agent to show you the interior. You only have two weeks to determine the condition of the property and decide if it's a good deal, and you'll have to determine how much you can afford to bid and arrange financing.

Two weeks isn't a long time to decide, so plan ahead. Select an area or several areas where you might want to bid and determine the property values in those areas. You will also want to have your financing arranged. This may mean qualifying for an FHA loan or a conventional loan or finding a partner. Since you only have forty-five days before you lose your bid and your deposit money, it's important to know that you can get the financing you need.

On some properties, often those needing some repairs, FHA financing is available to qualified buyers. If you're an owner-occupant, you'll get a break on the down payment. It can be as low as 3 percent. Even if you're buying as an investor, the down payment still can be as low as 15 percent.

VA REPOSSESSED PROPERTY SALES

Most people are aware that the VA helps people who have served in the armed forces to buy a home. These loans are usually made with no down payment and at a favorable interest rate. What the majority of the population doesn't know, though, is that many of these homes are available to anyone. You don't have to be a veteran, and you don't have to buy the property as a home for yourself. But you can

---
$$ MONEYMAKER $$

If you need a quick $17,500 to $48,000 to rehabilitate or upgrade your house or apartments, an FHA Title I loan can be obtained from a local mortgage broker or bank that deals with the federal government's Title I loan program. The interest rate is usually a couple of points above the prime rate, and the loan has some special characteristics. One is that it's easy to qualify for if you own your own home or another multiple rental property. The loan is for rehabilitation only, and you can do the work yourself and put cash in your pocket if you're handy with tools. The best part of this loan is that you don't have to have *any* equity in your property. You can buy a property today with 100 percent financing and get a Title I loan tomorrow to provide fix-up money and extra cash in your pocket.

---

still get a VA low-interest loan, and you can buy with a very small down payment or even none at all. You can even buy it for less than market price.

The secret to buying houses on such favorable terms is to look for VA repossessions. These "repos," as they're called, are houses that have been foreclosed on after the service men and women who bought them weren't able to make the payments.

Real estate brokers handle these sales, although you can buy direct from the VA without using a broker. Since the VA won't reduce the sales price if you don't use a broker, you might as well let a broker handle the details for you. It will save you time and trouble. The broker has to have signed up for the VA repo program and filed a signed copy of Form 26-8138 with the VA. This form simply states that the broker won't discriminate or be a party to discrimination based on race, color, religion, or national origin. To find a broker in your area who belongs to the VA repo program, simply call real estate offices and ask if they handle these properties.

The VA normally handles sales in the same way all over the country. Sometimes, if the VA has lots of houses that aren't selling in a particular district, it changes the policies to encourage sales. These changes are usually temporary but provide some good bargains while they last.

For instance, when the VA lists a house, they usually designate a list price and won't sell below that unless you pay all cash. But sometimes they waive the list price requirement and will accept lower offers. Also, there is usually a required 10 percent down payment, but when VA repos aren't selling well, the VA may waive the down payment requirement. The suit that was brought against the FHA will no doubt have repercussions on the VA, so by the time you read this things may have changed.

When you shop for VA repos, you have to be prepared—even more so than when buying HUD repossessed properties. You'll have only five working days to make an offer. First, you should have a good idea of property values for the area and the type of real estate you're interested in. Second, you should have your financing ready. Since preference is given to all-cash offers, you might want to form a partnership with several investors in order to be able to make a cash offer.

A typical VA listing includes the property address, a short description of the number of rooms, bedrooms, and baths, and the list price, along with information on the type of financing available, such as ''100 percent loan'' or ''$500 down.'' It will also state if the VA is accepting bids below list. Remember, there is usually a 10 percent down payment, unless you are a veteran and can use your entitlement for a no down payment loan. There is a 10 percent discount for all cash.

If you think the property will draw lots of bids because it's listed way below market value, or is in an excellent part of town, or you have a special reason for wanting to buy it, you can bid more than the list price. But remember, if you're buying for investment, it's not smart to get carried away and bid up the price. That's just a higher-priced version of ''auction fever.'' A better technique is to make more bids at list prices or, if allowed, below list price. You might have to make several offers before one is accepted, but it will be more profitable.

If you do decide to bid higher, you must bid a minimum of 3 percent above the list price. This amount is added to the down payment. When you can pay all cash, you can bid 10 percent lower than the list price.

The VA treats all offers received within five working days after

112

listing as though they arrived at the same time, unless all the offers meet all guidelines; then the earliest bid wins.

The guidelines the VA uses to decide the winning bid are, in this order:

1. **The highest all-cash offer.**
2. **The highest bid above the listed price.**
3. **If on terms, the amount of the cash down payment** when it exceeds the required down payment by 3 percent or more of the list price. The period of amortization is not a factor.
4. **Degree of acceptability of credit risk.**
5. **Purchase for own occupancy and use.**
6. **Veteran over nonveteran.**
7. **Earliest offer received** if offers are otherwise equal.

You will also have to prove to the VA that you have had two years of steady employment, have a three-month reserve of payments in the bank, and have good credit. The VA doesn't want the house back again.

$$ MONEYMAKER $$

Nathan found out the four-unit apartment building he lived in was being sold. He wanted to buy the building, but he had no money for a down payment, even though his income and the building's rents would have enabled him to meet the monthly payments. Then he learned that the owner, a veteran of World War II, would be happy to accept a no-down-payment offer from a qualified VA buyer.

Nathan knew the VA would finance one- to four-unit purchases for owner-occupant veterans. The problem was, he had never served in the armed forces. But his friend Jim *had* been in the service. So Nathan and Jim quickly formed a partnership that enabled them to buy the building with Jim's VA entitlement and Nathan's income.

After Jim moved into the building, the two friends embarked on a series of improvements that soon allowed them to raise rents on the other two units. Shortly afterward they sold the building for a handsome profit and bought a larger apartment complex that brought in enough income to support them both while they lived rent-free and concentrated their attention on further investment opportunities.

113

Those are some, but by no means all, of the opportunities to buy property with low prices and good terms from government sources. But there are also ways you can discover and bid at some remarkable government property auctions held in all parts of the country, where valuable real estate is often sold for a fraction of its true worth.

CHAPTER **11**

More Government Opportunities

Government real estate sources include more than FHA and VA programs and foreclosures. Several levels of government seize and sell real estate, as well as other property, to satisfy unpaid taxes or lawsuits. Personally I believe these types of sales yield some of the best bargains, because the government entity involved often has no interest in trying to sell the property for anywhere near its true value. Instead, the purpose of sale is merely to clear enough to pay off a lien or judgment. These are some auctions where you can find outstanding buys.

IRS LEVIED PROPERTY SALES

When business or individual federal taxes go unpaid for too long, the Internal Revenue Service (IRS) can serve the taxpayer with a notice and demand for payment and then wait ten days. If the money still isn't paid, the IRS can place a lien against any personal or real property the taxpayer owns, then levy against that property and sell it for money to cover the taxes.

With a few exceptions, the IRS can levy against virtually any property the taxpayer owns. You'd be amazed at what comes up on these sales. Paintings, cameras, furniture, cars, boats, jewelry, fur coats, office equipment, construction equipment, fine wines, hobby equipment, single-family homes, apartment buildings—if an American taxpayer can own it, the IRS can levy against it and sell it.

IRS levied property sales are handled under federal law, so they're similar all over the United States. The revenue officer responsible for each sale is in charge of notifying the general public. Some district or field offices of the IRS maintain a mailing list of people who are interested in bidding at levied property sales. Offices aren't required to do this, but many of them do.

You can contact field offices and district offices all over the country if you want, and ask to be on any mailing list they have. You can even ask to be on mailing lists for only certain kinds of levied property, depending on what you're interested in. Some IRS offices maintain separate lists for real and personal property, and the real property lists are sometimes even divided up for potential bidders on raw land, residential income property, commercial property, and so on. Offices that don't maintain a mailing list often have a special telephone number you can call for recorded information on upcoming sales.

Notices of IRS levied property sales must be published in a newspaper of general circulation in the same county where the property is located. Usually the IRS uses a legal newspaper for this, if there is one, although sometimes they advertise in the paper most people in the county subscribe to. Check both in the legal notices section and in the classified section under "Property Sales."

If there is no newspaper in general circulation in the county where the levied property is, the IRS will post the notices of sale in the nearest U.S. Post Office and at least two other public places. These notices will tell you what you need to know to decide whether or not to bid on the property or whom to contact for more information. They'll also tell you whether the sale will be a public auction or a sealed bid sale and the time and place of the auction or bid opening.

When you participate in a sealed bid sale, you generally have to include with your bid a deposit equal to 20 percent of your bid or $200, whichever is more. This money, and the money used to pay for your purchase if you are the high bidder, must be in the form of a certified check, cashier's or treasurer's check, or a money order.

There may be a minimum bid set for the sale. The revenue officer doesn't always reveal the minimum bid, however, until after the sale, although the person who owes the unpaid taxes must be told how much it is. According to the manual used by the IRS, the minimum bid should be figured at 80 percent of the forced sale value of the property, minus any loans or other outstanding encumbrances that have priority over the IRS lien.

The forced sale value is approximately 75 percent of the price that would bring a quick sale in a free market situation. This gets somewhat difficult to keep track of, so let's use an example to illustrate. Say the IRS levied against some vacant land worth about $50,000 in a free market. For a quick sale, a good price on this land would be $42,000. The forced sale value is 75 percent of the quick sale value; 75 percent of $42,000 is $31,500. The minimum bid is 80 percent of the forced sale value, so the minimum bid on this land would be $25,200—just over half the real value!

Value of land	=	$50,000
Quick sale value	=	$42,000
Forced sale value	=	75% of $42,000 = $31,500
Minimum bid	=	80% of $31,500 = $25,200

This is doubly attractive when you understand that many IRS levied property sales draw very few bidders, and the minimum bid often gets the property.

When you buy real property at an IRS levied property sale, you buy it subject to all prior encumbrances. This means that you assume responsibility for any mortgages, liens, or encumbrances against the property that were recorded *before* the date of the IRS lien. When any outstanding claims like these exist, the IRS subtracts those amounts from the minimum bid value. In our example of the vacant land above, if the taxpayer still owed someone $10,200 on the lot, the IRS minimum bid would drop down to $15,000.

If the highest bid equals or exceeds the minimum bid, the revenue officer in charge of the sale will declare the property sold to the highest bidder. At that point the winning bidder usually has thirty days to come up with the entire purchase price. A down payment, usually 20 percent of the high bid, has to be made right then. If it was a sealed bid auction, the deposit that came in with the bid will serve this purpose. If it was an oral auction, the winning bidder will have to be prepared with a certified check, cashier's or treasurer's check, or money order to hand over at the end of the bidding.

Occasionally, real estate sold at an IRS levied property auction will be redeemed by the previous owner or someone who has another lien against the property. They can do this up to 180 days after the sale. A certificate of sale is issued to the winning bidder when the purchase is made and the sale price paid; the deed itself is issued 180 days later, upon presentation of the certificate. If the property has been redeemed, however, the purchaser will get the full purchase price of the property from the person who is redeeming it, plus interest at the rate of 20 percent annually. There are very few investments that yield 20 percent—not CDs, not Treasury notes, not zero-coupon bonds, not money market funds, and certainly not your bank savings account. The payback with interest can amount to a nice profit even if you don't end up with the property.

SHERIFF'S SALES

Sheriff's sales are usually sales of property that has been levied against—either because the person or corporation didn't pay enough taxes to local or state revenue agencies or because of other legal debts. Courts have the authority to authorize sheriff's sales in their own localities.

Sheriff's sales can legally involve any and all property of the debtor, except for certain items that are protected from collection activities, such as in those states that allow a homestead exemption to be filed to protect the debtor's dwelling or where tools necessary to someone's primary occupation can't be levied against.

Sheriff's sales are also commonly used to sell real estate from mortgage foreclosures. When the mortgage payments fall too far behind, the lender will file a document called a *lis pendens*.

This notifies the owner and the court that the lender intends to ask for a judgment against the owner in order to foreclose on the mortgage.

After a waiting period, during which the owner has the opportunity to bring all payments up to date, there is a court hearing that usually results in a judgment. After this the lender can follow the same steps used by the winner of any lawsuit in demanding payment of the judgment and receiving a writ if payment isn't made. The sheriff is instructed to sell the property at auction to raise the money to satisfy the judgment.

Residential real estate, office buildings, income property, and vacant land often turn up at sheriff's sales. In addition, a great deal of business stock and equipment is auctioned off in sheriff's sales when businesses fail and their creditors sue for payment. During a recent one-month period I received several notices from one sheriff who was handling auctions of goods from a men's clothing store, a women's clothing store, an ice-cream parlor, a pizza restaurant, a bar, and two offices, among other things. Included on the lists of sale items were numerous lots of new clothing, office furniture and equipment, cases of liquor and soda, and a grand piano.

Whether the sale is the result of a lawsuit or a foreclosure, the sheriff schedules the auction and takes charge of all notifications. Notices must be posted where they can be easily seen on or near the property that will be sold, as well as in one public place within the judicial district.

In addition, a copy of the notice must be published in a newspaper for the city or judicial district where the property is located. This notice must run at least once a week during a twenty-day period. Copies of the notice have to be mailed to anyone who has recorded a request for notice from the court that issued the judgment, as well as to the person whose property is involved. These rules may vary in different jurisdictions, but there must always be public notification, a waiting period, and specific notification to directly interested parties.

Sheriff's sales are held as public oral auctions, and the property is sold to the highest bidder, who must pay the full price in cash, certified check, or money order and take possession immediately. Usually, but not always, the buyer of a bulky item like a car or a large piece of furniture will be given a short period of time to move it. The sale doesn't have to be confirmed by the court.

You can find out about sheriff's sales by checking the public notice boards at the courthouse or the sheriff's office, by watching the notices of sales in your local legal and regular newspapers, and by asking the sheriff to notify you. Usually sheriff's departments will accept self-addressed, stamped envelopes from people interested in being notified of a sale. Check with your local sheriff's department to find out the appropriate procedures for your area.

TAX SALES

All local communities need tax dollars to operate, and property taxes have long been the prime revenue source for counties and cities. When these tax bills go unpaid, local tax collectors can seize and auction the property.

In some states owners can reclaim, or redeem, property sold at tax sales by paying all back taxes, interest, and penalties within a redemption period. The length of the redemption period varies from state to state and may be anywhere from six months to five years. In other states owners lose the property with no right to redeem it; tax sales are final. We'll discuss this further in the sections about certificate and deed states later in this chapter.

The tax sale process starts with a certified letter notifying the property owner of overdue taxes. Some jurisdictions offer the property for sale at the very next auction, while others may let it ride for as long as five years or more before forcing a sale. Either way, public notice of intent to sell must be published in a local newspaper before any sale takes place. Quite often these notices appear in the cheapest newspaper with the lowest circulation, since the taxing authority tries to save money.

You can also contact the local tax collector or auditor and ask for a list of tax sale properties. This often comes as a computer printout that includes the name of the last property owner holding

—— **$$ MONEYMAKER $$** ——

It's often possible to pick up several parcels of raw land at a tax sale for prices as low as $25 each. Buy up as many of these as possible, get a realistic estimate of their true value, and add them to your financial statement as free-and-clear assets. Not only have you bought property that has instantly appreciated in value, but the addition to your net worth will look that much more attractive to lenders if you should ever apply for a loan. This property may also be used as collateral for loans or be traded as partial or full payment for improved property.

title, the legal description of the property including lot and block numbers, and the amount of back taxes and interest owed. The date, time, and place of sale also appear on the public notices and property lists.

Whether you consult published notices or receive your information directly from the taxing authority, you should take time to research any properties you're interested in before the sale. Check the title to see what other outstanding liens there may be and visit the site. Tax sale property is frequently raw land, but occasionally improved property comes up for bid. When it does, it's not always possible to see inside buildings, but you can inspect the exterior.

Oral bids are usually used for these sales, at which prices range from next to nothing to thousands of dollars, depending on the assessed value of the property and the number of years taxes have been in arrears. Payment requirements vary, although they always require cash or certified funds in some amount payable immediately upon purchase. For other important details of these sales, let's look at the differences between certificate states and deed states.

CERTIFICATE STATES

More than half the states fall into this category. They are listed on the next page. In these states buyers don't actually purchase title to the property at the tax sale. Rather, they buy the government's lien for back taxes.

CERTIFICATE STATES

Alabama	Montana
Arizona	Nebraska
Arkansas	New Hampshire
Colorado	New Jersey
Delaware	New York
Florida	North Carolina
Illinois	North Dakota
Indiana	Oklahoma
Iowa	South Carolina
Kentucky	South Dakota
Louisiana	Texas
Maryland	Wisconsin
Michigan	Wyoming
Minnesota	District of Columbia
Missouri	Puerto Rico

Property taxes are considered a lien on the property until they're paid, similar to a mortgage secured by a trust deed. The property tax lien is in first position and takes precedence over all other liens except for IRS liens. This means that if the property is foreclosed and sold, the property taxes are paid before any other indebtedness.

If you win the bid on a particular property in one of these states, the tax collector issues you a certificate. You hold this certificate through the redemption period—the grace period allowed the delinquent taxpayer to pay off the debt and reclaim the property.

Iowa, for example, allows taxpayers three years to redeem their property. If you bought a certificate in Iowa, the property's owner could go to the tax collector's office any time during the three years after the sale and pay the back taxes, along with a penalty and interest, and get the property back. You wouldn't lose, though. In fact, you'd gain. The tax agency would send you a check to redeem the certificate. You'd receive the back taxes, penalty, and interest.

If the owner fails to redeem the property by the end of the redemption period, you follow local procedures to gain title. In some places you foreclose on the lien you're holding, while in others you file a form with the tax collector and receive a deed.

It's important to learn the correct steps for your area so that you can file the proper forms and do whatever else is necessary to obtain title to properties on which you hold certificates. If you don't, you could lose your interest in the property.

Although the process may sound somewhat complicated, it becomes simpler as you get used to it, and it's well worth your while. You can pick up great bargains, and even if the property owner redeems the certificate, you can make a handsome profit from his penalties and interest. As an example, here are some interest rates on tax certificates:

- Indiana, 25 percent
- Illinois, 36 percent
- Louisiana, up to 41 percent
- Michigan, up to 50 percent

It would be difficult to find a better, safer investment. To learn the interest rate in your area, if you live in a certificate state, simply call the tax collector and ask.

Of course, if the owner doesn't redeem the certificate and you complete the process to receive title, you own the property. You can do as you please with it, just as you would with any other real estate you own. It's a no-lose proposition.

Some parcels at tax sales don't receive any bids, while others aren't bid high enough to pay off the back taxes. When this happens, the county, city, or state takes possession. This is also an opportunity worth exploring.

Government bodies don't want to manage property. They often negotiate private sales or hold public auctions to dispose of this real estate. If the government is holding property on which the redemption period has expired, you can purchase it and receive a deed immediately, even in a certificate state.

Tax sale certificates can be a uniquely profitable investment. The fact that very few people know about this opportunity makes it even better.

$$ MONEYMAKER $$

Pamela specializes in buying tax sales certificates from the states that pay the highest interest rates. She particularly likes the Michigan certificates that pay 50 percent. Her favorite technique is to buy the certificates six weeks or less before the redemption date. That way she can receive the greatest return on her money. A $2,300 Michigan certificate she bought recently was redeemed within four weeks and paid her nearly $3,500, which she considers is equal to an annual return of 600 percent on her investment. Using this strategy repeatedly, in some years she has realized as much as 1,000 percent returns.

DEED STATES

The major difference between tax sales in a certificate state and a deed state is that when you're the winning bidder in a deed state, you immediately receive a deed of ownership. The deed states are listed below. In most deed states the delinquent taxpayer has no right of redemption after the sale and the property is yours.

DEED STATES

Alaska	Ohio
California	Oregon
Connecticut	Pennsylvania
Georgia	Rhode Island
Hawaii	Tennessee
Idaho	Texas
Kansas	Utah
Maine	Vermont
Massachusetts	Virginia
Mississippi	Washington
Nevada	West Virginia
New Mexico	

There are no universal rules to this game, however, and a handful of deed states do allow a redemption period. You still receive interest if the property is redeemed, but you can't improve or sell the property during this time. These states include Georgia, Hawaii, Rhode Island, Texas, and Vermont. Arkansas allows a thirty-day redemption period. Some states permit a property owner a certain number of years during which to contest the validity of a tax sale in court. This is quite different from a right of redemption but is something you should ask about when investigating tax sale procedures in any locality.

Deed states present advantages and disadvantages. The process is simpler than the certificate procedures, and you do receive immediate title. On the other hand, when you buy in states that don't allow the previous owner to redeem his property after the tax sale, you miss out on the interest payments received by certificate holders when property is redeemed.

As in certificate states, when buying in deed states you should check with local county and property tax divisions to see if they conduct tax sales. If you find that property left over from these sales goes to the state, then you can also inquire at the state level about the availability of property.

Here is a brief summary of the similarities and differences between tax sales in certificate and deed states:

THE CERTIFICATE STATE	THE DEED STATE
• Information can be obtained at your local county or city property tax division.	• Same.
• Check with state about availability of property no one bid on.	• Same.
• Tax sale notice is published in a newspaper of general circulation.	• Same.
• Winning bid receives a tax certificate—not immediate ownership.	• Winning bid receives a deed and usually has immediate ownership.
• Property owner has right of redemption for a time.	• No right of redemption in most states; you're free to use property.
• Certificate will bear interest and penalty paid on redemption.	• No interest collected in states where redemption is not allowed.

Tax sales are a favorite investment of mine. The initial investment is low and the potential for profit is high. So few people take advantage of them, and I find so many uses for the land I acquire through tax sales, that at times I've practically regarded them as my own private bank.

CHAPTER **12**

Let Banks Make You Rich

When I speak of banks in relation to foreclosures, I include savings and loans, credit unions, private individuals, and any other entity that acts as a "bank" by carrying the mortgage or trust deed on a piece of real estate. When you know how to deal with them, banks are excellent sources of a seemingly endless supply of foreclosure properties.

If I had to choose one best real estate investment technique, I'd say, "Buy foreclosed property!" It offers the possibility of making the most money per deal of any method, because you can often buy well below market price. Dealing in foreclosures enables you to buy wholesale and sell retail. It can be a *very* profitable investment method. But, like anything else that offers the opportunity to make a lot of money, it requires that you know what you're doing.

Foreclosures are more complicated than normal real estate deals, so it is best to consult your attorney before attempting to make these investments. You can learn an enormous amount by talking to the people in the local tax office, but the foreclosure field is legally complex, so good legal counsel should be obtained on all aspects of the laws of your state and all applicable federal laws and regulations.

I'm not trying to scare you away from foreclosures; far from it.

I just want to encourage you to take the time to learn the laws and practices of your state. Laws and regulations, not to mention tax considerations, differ from state to state and are all subject to change.

You may have heard of investors who got in over their heads dealing in foreclosures and found themselves in trouble. Yes, that happens—to those who neglect to learn as much as they can about what they're doing and the laws involved. If you take the time to learn the ropes, you'll find that foreclosures are not terribly complicated. You've heard that knowledge is power, and nowhere is that statement more true than in dealing with foreclosed property. Learning all you can about foreclosures will give you the confidence to spot an opportunity and act on it decisively.

PROFIT FROM HELPING BANKS

Buying foreclosed properties from banks can be a good investment, for several reasons. Lenders don't want to own property. All they want is to get their money back—or to lose as little as possible. This often translates into a willingness to sell below market value—even for less than the amount of the foreclosed loan—in order to sell quickly and get as much money as possible back and into circulation again. A lender pays taxes and other expenses on a foreclosed property, and every month the property remains among the lender's assets, the cash it represents earns no interest. In other words, a foreclosed property "asset" is actually a financial drain on the lender.

You as the buyer, in most cases, are also dealing with a lender who has the power to approve the loan you use to take the property off his hands. Of course, you'll find different lenders show different levels of motivation. Some may not be smart enough to understand what could benefit them; others may look at the market and decide they can afford to wait for a better price. But in most cases you will find that you can buy good properties below market value and make a nice profit.

\$\$ MONEYMAKER \$\$

Tim found that the widespread crisis in the savings and loan industry created an opportunity windfall for investors. Since 1988 hundreds of banks and thrifts have been taken over and reorganized by the government because of mismanagement. One of the biggest problems with these failed financial institutions has been the large number of poor real estate loans they made that have been foreclosed and are being carried on the books as liabilities. These must be disposed of to put the lenders back on a sound financial footing.

Tim has bought some S and L foreclosure properties as cheaply as ten cents on the dollar. Although these are exceptionally good deals that don't turn up every day, Tim routinely buys properties at 50 percent of their true value. He finds them by contacting local offices of the Federal Deposit Insurance Corporation (FDIC) and Federal Savings and Loan Insurance Corporation (FSLIC) for property lists of real estate owned (REO).

NOT ALL FORECLOSURES ARE GOOD DEALS

Don't assume that a property is a good deal just because it's a foreclosure. It is always essential to evaluate the profit potential of any property before you buy. Don't neglect to do this, no matter how good the deal looks on the surface.

A friend tells a tale of a problem you might find. His real estate agent told him of this great deal on a house that was in foreclosure. My friend could buy it for only \$54,000. An inspection proved that it might have been a nice deal if the house were somewhere else and if the owner had treated it a little differently. It stood a block from a junkyard, was the largest house in a neighborhood of \$50,000 houses, and the inside had been nearly destroyed. It needed \$15,000 to \$20,000 worth of repairs just to make it livable, much less salable for top dollar, which in its location might have been about \$60,000.

Don't let that example discourage you, but use it as a warning. In whatever business employs you, do you let the fact that bad deals exist stop you from finding the good ones? Of course not. And I expect you to find more good deals in foreclosures than anywhere

129

else. The profits from just one good deal will more than justify the time you spend eliminating the bad ones.

FORECLOSURES ARE A FACT OF LIFE

You'll find that the number of foreclosures, and how profitable they are, vary according to the prosperity of the nation and of the immediate area. In the early and mid-1980s foreclosures reached a record level as the result of unemployment, changes in the job market, and, above all, high interest rates. By early 1989 prosperity had returned to most parts of the nation, and the interest rate was under 11 percent—but we still have foreclosures. There are not as many as there were a few years ago, but there are plenty to choose from. Whatever the economic circumstances, there are always some property owners who get into financial difficulty and can't meet their obligations.

Further, I believe that the early 1990s will see rising interest rates and a return to higher inflation, with the financial difficulties these conditions always bring in their wake. It probably won't get as bad as it did in the early 1980s, but the resulting wave of foreclosures will be almost as high.

I hate to see anyone suffer the pain of losing a house, losing money, and going through financial problems. That's the main reason I write books and lecture on ways people can improve their financial situations. Nevertheless, people do get into financial trouble, and there are foreclosures. There's not much you or I can do about it (except for a technique I'll tell you about in the next chapter). Once the bank takes over a property, it's not doing anyone any good. Then the best that can happen is that you or I or some other investor take the property off the bank's hands and put it back into productive use. To understand how to do that, let's take a closer look at foreclosures.

THE FORECLOSURE PROCEDURE

Even though the laws dealing with foreclosures differ in each state, there are two basic ways in which a property becomes the security

130

for money loaned on real estate. These are called, technically, "security devices," and one or both security devices may be used for real estate loans issued in your state.

The security device may be either a *mortgage* or a *trust deed*. There can be some confusion here, because in trust deed states a loan may still be called a mortgage, or a lender may call itself the "ABC Mortgage Company." What's important is whether you live in a "mortgage state" or a "trust deed" state. Below is a list of what states use which security device.

SECURITY DEVICES USED, BY STATE

STATE	SECURITY DEVICE
Alabama	Mortgage
Arizona	Deed of Trust
Alaska	Deed of Trust
Arkansas	Both
California	Deed of Trust
Colorado	Deed of Trust
Connecticut	Mortgage
Delaware	Mortgage
Florida	Mortgage
Georgia	Mortgage
Hawaii	Mortgage
Idaho	Deed of Trust
Illinois	Deed of Trust
Indiana	Mortgage
Iowa	Mortgage
Kansas	Mortgage
Kentucky	Both
Louisiana	Mortgage
Maine	Mortgage
Maryland	Both
Massachusetts	Mortgage
Michigan	Mortgage
Minnesota	Mortgage
Mississippi	Deed of Trust
Missouri	Deed of Trust
Montana	Deed of Trust

Nebraska	Deed of Trust
Nevada	Deed of Trust
New Hampshire	Mortgage
New Jersey	Mortgage
New Mexico	Deed of Trust
New York	Mortgage
North Carolina	Deed of Trust
North Dakota	Mortgage
Ohio	Mortgage
Oregon	Deed of Trust
Pennsylvania	Mortgage
Rhode Island	Mortgage
South Carolina	Mortgage
South Dakota	Mortgage
Tennessee	Deed of Trust
Texas	Deed of Trust
Utah	Deed of Trust
Vermont	Mortgage
Washington	Deed of Trust
West Virginia	Deed of Trust
Wisconsin	Mortgage
Wyoming	Mortgage

When someone stops making payments on a loan or breaks some term of the loan agreement, the bank has recourse to a foreclosure action to recover the money. Note that the law does not require a lender to foreclose but does spell out the conditions under which foreclosure may take place and how it shall be done.

LEARN THE PROCEDURE IN YOUR STATE

The first thing you should do when you decide to go into the foreclosure business is get a thorough knowledge of the exact process in your state. There are several sources for this information.

In title companies, the chief title officer is responsible for knowing all the legalities involved in title transfers, which of course includes foreclosure. In some states he or she, or a designated assistant, should be able to tell you all you need to know, and more,

132

and it won't cost you anything. In other states title companies do not cooperate in giving people this information. Ask. If they'll work with you, they should be an authoritative source. If they won't, there are other sources.

Real estate brokers and agents should know about foreclosures, but if they don't make a specialty of them, they may not know about them or may not know everything. At minimum, they should be able to get the information for you or tell you where to get it. They don't cost anything, either, until they close a deal for you and make their commission.

A lender may be able to help you with loan requirements for foreclosures, especially if you are dealing with a foreclosure that is one of that lender's REOs (real estate owned). The lender may offer you a favorable interest rate to take the property off his hands. You may have to ask, and negotiate, and keep making counteroffers to get everything a lender is willing to give. I can't say it often enough: If you don't ask, you won't get.

Finally, don't hesitate to check with an attorney. This may be especially important in mortgage states, where foreclosures are handled by attorneys as legal proceedings. You'll want to know what local practice is and how to be sure you follow the rules. An attorney will charge for consultation, but this is money well spent. To play the foreclosure game, you must know the rules; once you do, your profits will more than repay the cost of acquiring the knowledge.

To start you on your way, I'll give you a brief overview of the different procedures used in mortgage and trust deed foreclosures.

THE MORTGAGE DEFAULT PROCESS

Judicial foreclosure is usually employed where mortgages are the security device. The mortgage holder files a lawsuit against the borrower in the courts. There must be a judicial finding of default on the loan before the lender can take over the title to the property and sell it to satisfy the debt. Attorneys handle the action.

When a foreclosure goes through the courts, the case will take months, perhaps a year or more. Courts at their most efficient

---
$$ MONEYMAKER $$

Brad, Ralph, and Tim formed a partnership to buy foreclosure properties. Banks in their area would only loan up to 80 percent of the purchase price rather than 80 percent of the full value of property bought below market value. For instance, if Brad bought a property worth $90,000 for $60,000, the bank would only loan 80 percent of $60,000, or $48,000, on the property. This made it difficult for the partners to refinance their foreclosure bargains for enough money to continue investing.

Then the lawyer in the group came up with a perfectly legal loophole. Tim supplied the cash, and Brad and Ralph bid and bought properties far under market value in their own names. They then signed the properties over to Tim at full market price. With a purchase contract showing that he was paying full market value, Tim was able to obtain 80 percent bank financing on the full worth of the property.

So, Brad bought a $90,000 property for $60,000, which he then signed over to Tim at the full $90,000 value. Brad accepted Tim's note for $18,000 as the down payment, and Tim financed 80 percent of his purchase price, or $72,000, through the bank. Tim then gave Brad the $72,000 he had borrowed from the bank to use in buying more foreclosure property. Using this method, the three friends were able to raise the cash to acquire many more properties than they could have if they had simply refinanced based on the foreclosure sale price.

---

move slowly, and they often have a long backlog of cases. Just how long a foreclosure action takes in your state or city will depend on the requirements and complexity of local law and the court backlog.

During the judicial process the lender receives no payments— not one dime—and must pay legal fees, too. During that time, in accordance with state law, the property owner has the opportunity to redeem, or bring the payments current on, the property. Failing that, the court finally releases the property to the lender, and the lender can offer it for sale using methods similar to those you'll find described for the deed of trust.

STEPS IN A FORECLOSURE: A TRUST DEED STATE

Foreclosure involving a deed of trust takes much less time than a mortgage foreclosure. It can be over in as little as a month. Again, each state is different. You should find a basic similarity among trust deed states, but details will differ. There may be extra steps or fewer steps in your state, and time limits will vary.

Foreclosure in a trust deed state is a nonjudicial action. It does not go through the courts. There cannot be a deficiency judgment against the trustor (borrower). The lender can only go to the property to get his or her money back.

Step One

At the time the property is purchased, the trustor/borrower executes a note promising to repay the loan under specified conditions. Usually the borrower only worries about how much the payment is and what day of the month it's due; but of course the note is a contract that contains a lot more than that, including the conditions under which the note will be deemed to be in default and foreclosure may be started.

The beneficiary (lender) receives a note secured by a deed of trust. The actual deed is held by a trustee, a neutral third party. (This is one thing that makes a trust deed state different from a mortgage state; in a mortgage state the deed is held directly by the beneficiary/lender.)

Everything is fine as long as the trustor/borrower fulfills the terms of the note. When conditions aren't met, the process moves to step two.

Step Two

The borrower can be considered in default for violating any terms of the loan agreement, but most commonly for

1. Falling behind in monthly payments
2. Failing to make monthly payments by the agreed date

3. Failing to make a balloon payment when due
4. Becoming delinquent in payment of taxes or insurance

When any of these things happen, the beneficiary/lender instructs the trustee to begin foreclosure proceedings. A prescribed minimum amount of time must elapse before the trustor/borrower can be considered in default (the length of time may be controlled by state law or may be written into the loan contract and will vary widely). A beneficiary/lender has the option of waiting longer than the minimum time if he or she wishes to or feels the borrower can bring the loan current.

Step Three

After the lender contacts the trustee and informs him or her of the default, the trustee prepares a Notice of Default. This states the reasons for the default and the amount of money needed to cure the default (bring the account current) or the actions that must be taken to abide by the terms of the contract.

The Notice of Default is recorded at the county courthouse, and the trustee mails a Notice of Default to the trustor/borrower. In California the mailing to the trustor/borrower must take place within ten days of recording the notice. Check your state laws.

If there are junior lien holders (second or third loans, mechanic's liens, IRS or tax liens) whose liens would be eliminated by the foreclosure, they must be notified (within thirty days in California).

Step Four

Now the trustor/borrower must respond or the foreclosure will proceed. The trustor/borrower can, at any time (within three months of the Notice of Default in California or other lengths of time set by other state law), redeem the loan delinquency and remove the default by paying

1. All delinquent payments
2. Costs incurred by the beneficiary/lender, such as taxes, insurance, and interest
3. Costs incurred by the trustee (trustee fees)

If the trustor/borrower does this, the foreclosure proceeding stops, and everything is as if it had never happened.

Step Five

If, however, the trustor/borrower cannot bring the loan current and pay all fees, the final foreclosure process begins. The beneficiary instructs the trustee to set a date for the sale of the property and to make the formal publications required by law to advertise the public sale of the property. This Notice of Sale will include

- The time and place of the sale
- Address and legal description of the property
- The names of all parties involved
- The address and phone number of the trustee
- The amount owed (the unpaid obligation)

Publication must be in a "newspaper of general circulation" in the judicial district in which the about-to-be-foreclosed property is located. This is not always the largest paper but is often the smallest paper that meets the legal requirements.

The trustee sets the date of sale as required by law—in California, at least twenty-one days after the first day of publication. The trustee then mails a Notice of Sale to all parties who have been sent the original Notice of Default. If the owner has a federal tax lien against him or her, the trustee mails a special notice to the IRS.

Watch for IRS Liens

The IRS must be notified twenty-five days prior to the sale and has 120 days to redeem the sale. The IRS must pay the amount of the sale price (the price actually paid when the property is sold) in order to redeem the property.

This is important. You may buy a property that has an IRS lien on it, but unless you pay off the lien you cannot be certain it is yours until the 120 days after notification for the IRS has passed. This would make a difference if you needed to resell quickly to make your profit or could not afford to have your money tied up while you waited for the IRS to make up its mind. If the IRS decides to redeem the property, the winning bidder (you or I) must pay the tax lien, whatever it was, to secure his or her interest in the property and remove the IRS from the picture.

If you're interested in a property, call the IRS and ask whether there is a lien against the owner. An IRS tax lien against the owner may not yet be recorded against the property, but the IRS can do so if it chooses. You may find someone willing to tell you whether the IRS has any interest in the property or whether the IRS will go after it if the property is sold.

When One Property Carries Multiple Loans

If the first loan holder forecloses, junior loans are wiped out by the foreclosure. If a second loan holder forecloses, he or she would have to bring current and assume the first loan. Third or fourth loans would then be wiped out, unless those loan holders found it worthwhile to assume and bring current the loans ahead of them.

In practice, third and fourth loans often overencumber the property, and the holders of those loans (who usually have charged high interest because of their high risk) may find that they lose less money by giving up the loan than by foreclosing.

Anyone who has a mechanic's lien on the property is notified of the sale and may either bring the payments current or bid at the sale. Otherwise their lien is wiped out at the time of sale. It is rare for the holder of a mechanic's lien to foreclose, but it happens.

The trustor/borrower has the right to pay off the loan, and all unpaid interest and costs, at any time up to the sale.

Step Six

At the advertised date, time, and place of sale, the trustee puts the property up for bid. The beneficiary always has the first bid. Usually, but not always, the beneficiary's representative bids the amount owed, plus costs and interest. The beneficiary does not have to be present to bid but may so instruct the trustee.

The trustee may ask for additional bids. Any bidder must produce cash or a cashier's check in the amount of the bid and show it to the trustee before the trustee accepts the bid. Evidence of a loan commitment may be accepted as equivalent to ''cash.'' (Check the requirements.) The successful bidder then owns the property.

The buyer takes title to the property subject only to those liens that were on record *prior* to recordation of the deed of trust that secured the foreclosed loan (except for IRS liens, as described above).

Right of Redemption

Once the sale is made (in California), there are no other rights of redemption. The original trustor/borrower has no further rights, and the foreclosure is recorded in the county courthouse and upon his or her credit record.

Some states allow periods following the sale in which the original trustor/borrower can reclaim the property by paying the entire amount of the loan, including delinquent payments, and all costs of sale and legal fees, plus interest.

BANK REOS

Bank REOs (real estate owned) are a different ball game. These are properties that have been foreclosed and were not sold at the public sale. The bank now owns this real estate and may dispose of it in any way it sees fit. Rules are set by the individual banks, and they're not bound by the kinds of government regulations that affect FHA and VA foreclosures.

139

They are, of course, bound by the government banking regulations that govern all lending. They're competing in the market on the same basis as anyone else trying to sell a property and are limited only by the same real estate laws that affect everyone else. As a result, you'll find banks that are very motivated to get rid of those properties, banks that don't seem to really care, and all attitudes in between.

To start with, assume the bank you walk into is a motivated seller. If it turns out that that particular bank isn't, or if it doesn't happen to have any REOs in your area, go to the next bank.

Once you find a cooperative lender with REOs in your area, treat the properties like any other deal you'd make. Decide whether you want a particular property, what it's worth, and what you think the bank will accept. Chances are, if you offer something near what the bank expects to get, you've got a deal.

Then you ask for good financing. If the bank is going to give a good loan to anyone, it will give one to someone taking a REO off its hands.

Locating REOs

There are enough banks and S&Ls in most areas to make it time-consuming to visit each of them every couple of weeks or months looking for what's new on their lists. One way to keep track is to talk to the loan officer, explain what you're looking for, and ask him or her to call you when something comes onto the list. If the loan officer is doing his job, he'll call.

The bank might prefer to put you on a mailing list, if it has one. Or the loan officer could suggest that you telephone every so often to ask what's new. You're likely to find as many responses as there are banks and S&Ls. If you work on these relationships, you may get a chance to make an offer on a REO before others know it is available.

If that seems like a lot of work (it is) and you don't have time to do it, there are other ways. A real estate agent who works FHA and VA foreclosures may also keep track of REOs. Let the agent do

140

it. Sometimes REOs show up in the real estate classified ads. Keep on the lookout for them.

In some cities foreclosure services, for a fee, publish lists of REOs. If there's such a service in your area, you'll probably find it advertised in the real estate classifieds or sometimes in the Sunday real estate section of your paper or the Sunday paper in the nearest major city. Such a list, if the publisher has done a good job, can save you a lot of walking, driving, or telephoning. Remember, however, that when a property is listed by a foreclosure service, you'll have to compete for the best buys against everyone else who subscribes to the service. Scan the list as soon as you receive it and be ready to act quickly if you find a property that appeals to you.

You might think there would be no government financing for bank REOs, but if you and the property qualify for FHA or VA financing, the bank or S&L will be very happy to make the loan and help you get it.

In my opinion, bank foreclosures are among the best ways—if not *the* best way—to build your investment nest egg through real estate. Profits from the resale of one foreclosure bargain can be invested in another and another, until you're on your way to financial independence.

141

CHAPTER **13**

Help Yourself by Helping Others

You can find excellent real estate bargains when you're able to buy a piece of property after the owner has gone into default on his loan but before the foreclosure takes place. This is a true win-win situation in which you can help people who are about to lose their property and both parties end up better off than if the foreclosure went through. You get a good price on a property, maybe the best possible price, and the owner doesn't lose everything. Usually even the lender is happy to avoid going through foreclosure.

To bring about this happy ending, you need three things. First, the owner must have enough equity in the property that you can offer to bring the loan current and pay it off and still get a good deal.

Second, the owner must be realistic enough to be willing to negotiate in order to avoid foreclosure. Believe it or not, some people will lose their homes to foreclosure rather than yield on price and make a deal that would save them a blot on their credit record. If you run into them, you can neither help them nor make money.

Third, you have to find those owners who have enough equity and who are willing to deal with you in time to make the offer.

Now, the first two conditions are pretty obvious. But how do you find them?

FORECLOSURES ARE PUBLIC INFORMATION

Foreclosures are legal matters, recorded at the county courthouse, and notice must be published in a "newspaper of general circulation." Filings at the courthouse are a matter of public record, which means you have a right to see them. Simply go to the courthouse (or phone) and ask who keeps those records and how you go about seeing them.

These records are usually kept by the county recorder or county clerk, or someone with a similar title. The title may vary according to state law and practice. If you call the "information" number in your county government listings at the front of your phone book, they'll tell you. If there isn't an information number, and you're not sure which department is the right one, make a guess and call. If you're wrong, you'll be told whom to call.

When you find the correct office, try to make friends with someone there. Although the information you're looking for is public record, not many people exercise their right to see it. Employees of the office are used to attorneys, lenders, and title company people looking at the records, but not, usually, other citizens. So explain who you are, what you want to do, and why it's important for you to get the information as soon as possible.

You may find that they write up the week's foreclosures at certain intervals or on certain days, and if they make copies of the result, you can ask them to make one for you. They're not required to make you a copy, but if you've made a friend, you may be able to get one. It's easier than looking through the actual original filing records and should be easier for the person in the office, too. Expect to pay for copies, at whatever rate they charge. (If you can get a copy, it probably means they make copies for attorneys, too, for a fee.)

The key is to cooperate with your county employees and be pleasant and convince them to cooperate with you. The only time to be demanding is when you encounter someone who denies you your right to see public record information. It doesn't happen often, but if it does, be polite. Ask to see the person's boss. If that fails, try your county attorney's office (another title that may be different in

144

different jurisdictions). As a last resort, consult an attorney and take whatever legal action is needed.

If you can't or don't want to take the time to go to the courthouse, find out which newspaper publishes the legal notices of foreclosure and on what day. It may not be the major paper in the county, because the usual legal requirement is only "a newspaper of general circulation," so the county will normally put its legal advertising in the cheapest paper that meets the requirement.

The catch is that if you wait for newspaper advertising, you've wasted time in which you could have made a deal with the owner. The foreclosure is not advertised when the Notice of Default is filed, but when the redemption period has expired without the borrower bringing the loan current. At that point the advertisement must run for three weeks, after which the sale may be held.

APPROACHING OWNERS IN FORECLOSURE

Find out who is in foreclosure from the public records, then do your usual evaluation of the price, the house, the neighborhood, and so on. Eliminate properties that are overencumbered or that, for whatever reason, you would not wish to own anyway. You'll be left with those that look good on paper and on a drive-by inspection. Write to the owner, explaining who you are, sympathizing with his plight, and offering your help.

The letter might read something like this:

Dear Mr. and Mrs. Owner:

I have seen the legal Notice of Default showing that your home loan is in default and that foreclosure proceedings have begun. It is my sincere hope that you will be able to redeem your loan and keep your home.

If you feel that this might not be possible, I would like to talk with you about purchasing your home, which would save you from a foreclosure proceeding and keep the foreclosure off your credit record.

I am a real estate investor, and if your home fits the needs of my portfolio, I would be pleased to negotiate for purchase at a fair price.

145

Please contact me at the above address, or phone 000-0000.

Sincerely,

Joseph Investor

Of course, this won't always work. People under pressure don't always behave with their usual good sense. In fact, people who receive a notice telling them that their loan is in default and that they may lose their home often go into a period of denial. They may ignore the notice, may not tell their spouse, and may act as if the problem will somehow go away if they pretend it doesn't exist. Someone who is behind in house payments almost always has additional financial and other problems: perhaps loss of a job, overwhelming medical bills, or a marriage on the rocks. List all the bad things that can happen to good people, and you can expect to find some combination of them in the person facing foreclosure.

Be sensitive to the pain and distress that this person is feeling, and be caring about their problems—but not too caring. You're not a social worker, and you're not a government agency with money to spend. You can't let yourself "help" foreclosure families just because they're nice, deserving people—unless you've made so many millions you can become a philanthropist and give away money.

The important thing is to convey the message that you care. It will make negotiations easier and will help the person to recover from the shock of losing a home and to pursue a course of action that will benefit both of you. Just never forget, and never let the person forget, that you can help only if you make money. Remember that you're an investor; identify yourself to the people as an investor. They know investors expect to make money.

LET OWNERS FIND YOU

Another way to find foreclosures, sometimes even before a foreclosure is filed, is to run an ad that might read something like this:

Behind on your home loan payments? I'm interested in buying your home at a fair price. Call Dave, 000-0000.

146

━━━ $$ MONEYMAKER $$ ━━━

Clark has enlisted his friends to help him find owners who are about to go into foreclosure. Clark has observed that these owners often neglect their property as their troubles mount. His friends carry printed cards that say, "Financial problems? Maybe I can help. Talk to me about buying your house." Clark's name and phone number follow.

Whenever one of Clark's friends notices a house showing signs of neglect, he places one of these cards on the gate or the front door or someplace where it will be noticed. Clark has made several good deals from contacts made this way, and the friend responsible gets a 5 percent interest in the property.

This ad should run in the rental section of the classified ads, because someone who can't make payments and faces foreclosure will want to be renting, not buying another home.

Your ad may find sellers who know they're in trouble—perhaps one of them has lost a job—but who have not yet missed enough payments to bring on foreclosure. Such sellers will usually be extremely motivated. It will certainly turn up sellers who are looking for a place to rent because foreclosure is developing and they can't do anything about it. You might even have a property for rent that they could afford. Just be sure they would make good, responsible tenants before you mention the possibility.

Once you have found a foreclosure before the sale, you can deal with the owners as you would with any other sellers—except that these sellers should have exceptionally powerful motivation and should be treated a little more carefully and sensitively because of the emotional pain they're going through. When you meet with these sellers, don't try high-pressure tactics on them, and don't try to take undue advantage. Taking unfair advantage of distressed sellers is not only immoral, in many states it's specifically illegal. Later, when the financial pressure is off, these people could decide you cheated them when their backs were to the wall. If a judge agrees with them, you'll have legal problems on your hands.

What you can do, though, is offer them a fair discounted price. For example, say their house is worth about $80,000 in a neighborhood where the general price range is $77,000 to $83,000 for similar homes. They bought their house five years ago for $75,000 and refinanced it once. Their current loan balance is $71,000 at 10 percent interest with a monthly payment of $675 including taxes and insurance. Back payments and late charges total $2,100. It looks like this:

Value of house	$80,000
Mortgage	$71,000
Back payments	$ 2,100

You can offer them this: Since no real estate agent is involved, you deduct the amount of the house's full price that would go to pay a real estate commission. For a 6 percent commission, that would be $4,800. Then, since you will make up the back payments for them, deduct another $2,100, for a total of $6,900.

Value of house	$80,000
Commission	− 4,800
Back payments	− 2,100
Final price	$73,100
Loan balance	− 71,000
Sellers receive	$2,100

Instead of being $2,100 behind and facing foreclosure, the sellers are out of debt, have saved their credit rating, and receive enough cash to make a deposit on a rental home or pay off some other bills. You've picked up a property for $7,000 less than its market value. You'll probably have to pay some closing costs and perhaps loan fees or points if you can't assume their old loan. But you'd have to pay those in any case, and you're still getting the house at a bargain price.

You can use the house as a rental, holding it while prices rise, or resell immediately for full value. But that's only the beginning. I have a great deal of information yet to share with you on ways to increase your profits, multiply the funds available for your investment plan, and just generally make nothing but money.

148

PART III

Wealth Multipliers

CHAPTER 14

Use Credit and Partnerships to Increase Profit Growth

The more money you invest, the more profits you receive; the more profits you earn, the more money you have to invest. That's the profit spiral I mentioned earlier, and it's the one sure way to increase wealth. Simply start out with whatever assets you have, then use the investment techniques I have described to take you toward whatever financial goal you set.

Sometimes, though, people want to reach financial independence more quickly or don't have enough cash to invest in a wonderful opportunity that comes their way. But don't give up. There are techniques to enable you to increase your profits beyond what your cash reserves would normally allow.

One is to use credit. I'm usually conservative when it comes to using credit, because I believe charging everything you want is an excellent way to spend yourself into poverty. However, when you have thought out how you plan to pay back your credit, and then discipline yourself to stick to the plan, loans and charge cards can be valuable tools for building wealth.

For example, you might learn of a valuable lot of jewelry coming up for auction. The minimum bid is $3,000, and a careful inspection at the preview convinces you that you could sell the entire lot for at least $10,000. The only problem is, your cash reserve is less than $2,000 right now. Since you're positive that you can sell the jewelry, set yourself a maximum bid, such as $6,000, and borrow that amount. Use a loan, take out advances against credit cards, or ask another person to come in as your partner for a share of the profits.

The day of the auction, you arrive with your $6,000 in hand and enter the bidding. If it goes above $6,000, you would drop out, since you don't want to exceed your maximum. Let's say, though, that you make the successful bid at $5,500. Don't waste time. Resell the jewelry in the shortest possible amount of time. With the profits, immediately pay back your loan or your partner.

What if your original estimate was slightly optimistic and you receive only $9,000 for the jewelry? Since you didn't exceed your maximum bid, that leaves you plenty of room to pay back your purchase loan or pay off your credit cards, along with any interest and fees, and still nets you an excellent profit. If you're splitting with a partner, each of you receives a good return.

Whatever profit you make should be kept in a special account and not spent except to invest in other profit-earning ventures. Above all, I cannot emphasize too strongly the importance of paying back loans and partners first, before you do anything else with your money. This frees your credit for future deals and impresses anyone who goes into partnership with you. As you move into larger investments such as real estate, you'll need good credit and favorable references.

Many people, especially those with poor credit of their own, find partners invaluable in any plan to build wealth. You can improve your credit application without drastic changes in your income or assets by finding someone (or several people) willing to combine their financial statement(s) with yours. Usually the partner(s) also combine their cash with yours. You may find partners who will put up all the money needed in exchange for your time and effort in locating good investment properties.

These people can be such important factors in your success that it's time to examine partnerships more closely. Since I'm such a strong advocate of real estate, we'll look at partners in that context, but you can invite them to join you in almost any legal investment activity.

$$ MONEYMAKER $$

Chuck and Maria often found that their mail contained applications for credit cards with preapproved cash advances. They always threw them out, since they thought they had enough credit cards and didn't want to pay annual fees for nothing. They were sure their $50,000 home equity line of credit (HEL) would cover any quick cash needs they might have.

Then they found an opportunity to buy an office complex worth $1.2 million for $750,000, which would be carried by the seller, if they could come up with $150,000 cash. Chuck and Maria started applying for every card with a preapproved credit line that they could find. Each applied separately, and they also applied for cards in the name of their business. They were able to obtain twenty cards with average limits of $5,000 for a total of $100,000 of unsecured credit. Added to their HEL, it was enough to buy the office complex.

Income from the office complex covered all their payments, and a few months later Chuck and Maria sold the complex for a nice profit of close to half a million dollars in addition to the money to pay off all their credit balances. Chuck and Maria now realize that $100,000 worth of unsecured credit card loans will help them become millionaires very quickly.

QUALITIES OF A GOOD PARTNER

You're looking for a partner who will complement your strengths; that is, his or her strengths will compensate for areas where you are weak, and your strengths will compensate for areas in which the partner is weak.

A typical example would be if you had little money but were willing to take the time to research real estate values and market considerations. Your contribution to the partnership would be to find properties that would provide a good return on investment. If needed, you can and will take the time to rehabilitate, or supervise the rehabilitation, of properties that need it.

These are considerable strengths and very valuable to a partnership. To complement your strengths, you need someone who has money but is too busy to pursue investment; or the potential partner may be neither sufficiently interested nor motivated. He or she may not want to take the time to find a place to invest that provides something better than the low yield of CDs and the high risk of stocks. People like this may be very happy to have someone else (you) do the work that enables them to make money.

If I have decent credit, but limited assets and not much cash flow, and time to do the investment work, while you have assets and a lot of cash flow, but lack the time, we'd make a good team, wouldn't we? Of course we would.

Now, you may wonder how far this can go. Suppose you have no job, no assets, no money, no credit, no nothing; can your partner use his whole financial statement to get a loan for both of you? Can your partner put up *all* the money for the deal after you go out and find the property?

Yes. The mortgage lender is interested in the *total* assets and liabilities of the partnership, not what one partner or the other brings to it. In short, you provide motivation, knowledge, and time, while your partner provides money and a good financial statement.

━━━ $$ MONEYMAKER $$ ━━━

OPC—other people's credit or financial statement—can make the difference in closing a deal. Belinda found a property worth $80,000 that she could buy for $68,000 because the seller had moved to another state and wanted to get out from under double house payments. Belinda had enough cash for the $7,300 down payment and her share of closing costs, but no credit record, so she couldn't qualify on her own for a loan to purchase the property. Inquiries among all her friends and relatives turned up Rick, a cousin she barely knew, who was willing to become her partner and let Belinda use his excellent credit background to obtain the necessary loan. When they resold the property for a $12,000 profit six months later, Belinda kept 70 percent because she had found the deal and done all the work, while Rick received 30 percent for allowing Belinda to use his credit. Belinda was pleased to make $8,400, well over and above the $7,300 she had put in as down payment and to cover closing costs, and Rick felt his $3,600 was ample return for nothing more than filling out a financial statement and signing a few papers.

154

USING PARTNERSHIP ASSETS

Many people ask how you combine your financial statement with that of a partner when applying for loans. On any credit application you'll see that where they ask for your name there is a space for "co-borrower." On many property purchases that will be the spouse of the borrower, but it doesn't have to be. It can just as well be a partner. You will usually show your assets and the partner's in separate lists, unless you have formed a company or made a legal partnership agreement. For a company or legal partnership, provide a statement of combined assets.

I should also note that you don't have to be limited to the spaces provided on a bank form. If you have carefully designed your financial statement to answer all the questions on the form, you can simply write: "See attached financial statement." Provide a nicely prepared listing of your assets and liabilities typed on a good typewriter or typeset by a computer with a desktop publishing program.

If you don't own a computer with a letter-quality or laser printer, or a good typewriter, look in the Yellow Pages for a secretarial or word-processing service and have them do it. A word-processing or secretarial service using a computer is best. Those using laser printers can make your financial statement look very attractive. When they've done your statement they can store it on a disk, and whenever you need it again they can run you another few copies.

FINDING PARTNERS

Now the major question is, where can you find prosperous partners with good financial statements? Actually they're all around you. Take a look at other cars on the road next time you drive down to the supermarket or shopping mall. How many Mercedes, BMWs, Jaguars, Porsches, Continentals, and Cadillacs do you see? You can figure that for every expensive car on the road, someone is earning enough money to be an excellent partner.

I'll tell you one technique I've used to find the people driving those expensive automobiles. I've written a letter to every doctor and dentist in the Yellow Pages. What I said, basically, was

155

Hi! I'm Dave Del Dotto. I'm a real estate investor, and I've bought and sold millions of dollars' worth of property. I've helped many doctors like yourself build impressive real estate investment port-folios. If you're interested in a good return on your money and substantial tax savings, I'd like to talk to you.

Pretty soon I'd get letters or phone calls from more people than I could find time to work with. If you know any doctors, you understand why. Most of these men and women are dedicated workaholics who just don't have much time to do anything but take care of our colds and cavities. When they do have spare time, they don't want to work on some other project; they want to go to Hawaii, Acapulco, Vail, or Europe and relax—and I don't blame them. I would, too, if I worked in one of their professions.

The same is true of many other professions, to varying degrees. You'll find that business executives often put in ten- to twelve-hour days, plus weekends, and have money to spend but no time to invest it. The key is to figure out who has money but no time and seek out those people.

Sending out a large mailing to prospects might result in fifty people calling you back wanting to invest their money (depending on how big your town is, how many people you send mailings to, and other factors). But suppose you just want one good partner, quickly, to make one good deal that you've located but can't handle yourself?

USE A CREATIVE APPROACH

Chances are that you know personally a few people who have money or perhaps people who know someone else who'd be interested. Try that route first. If it doesn't produce a partner, you could try something a little different.

Make an appointment with your doctor, if you've known him or her long enough. When he comes into the examining room and asks what seems to be the trouble, say something like "I'm terribly depressed, and I hope you can cure me, because I've got this great deal lined up, and with the right partner, I could make 25,000 bucks and so could my partner. Doc, how'd you like to be my partner?"

Don't wait for him to get over his shock; tell him about the deal. He should be surprised and flattered that you were willing to spend the price of an appointment to offer him a chance to make money without having to work for it. Be confident; don't try to describe the deal in detail or get a commitment on the spot (unless you see that you can, for certain; always be ready to close a deal when you see the chance). Plan to get him interested and set up a meeting so you can show him the figures and the property.

That's a variation on one of the oldest techniques in business. It's called various things, like networking, using your contacts, rewarding your friends, and so on.

LET CONTACTS HELP YOU—AND THEMSELVES

When I was a kid, everybody understood that if you were in business, you learned to play golf. The country club golf course was where you met other businessmen on an informal basis, making friends and contacts. Everyone knew that you did business through friends and contacts. Today, the country club is still important, but there are many more places where business contacts are made, and that's to our advantage. You don't have to become part of the country club set.

The secret of making partnerships is making contacts. You can do it by mailing to good prospects, or you can do it by talking to all the people you know—you'll be surprised how many contacts you have that you've never thought of. Are you a member of a church? Do you work on church committees? Chances are you know people who have money.

Don't be afraid to ask someone you already know. The person you know at church (or at work, school, in a service club, at the gym or aerobics class; wherever) may know someone else who is interested if he or she doesn't want to invest. I've made lots of deals because I knew someone who knew someone, and so on.

You need to master this contact-developing technique if you're going to use partnerships successfully to amass wealth. If you try to do everything alone, it will slow you down. There are so many deals out there, and so many potential partners, that the more partners you can find and the more property you can buy, the wealthier you will become.

EXPANDING YOUR NETWORK

When you've never thought about building a network of investment contacts before, where to start can seem like a mystery. The first step is getting out and meeting people. Think about the kinds of activities that appeal to those with money. Charity committees, political organizations, and business associations are good places to start. Check the business and society pages of your newspaper and make note of functions attended by local movers and shakers.

If you have children, or like to work with them, youth activities can form a natural meeting ground. Children of bankers, attorneys, and other well-off professionals play soccer and Little League and join the Girl Scouts.

As you begin to meet people, don't hit them over the head with your ideas to build wealth, but don't hide the facts, either. Work on becoming known as a friendly, reliable person before you approach people for money. Talk enthusiastically about your goals when the subject forms a natural part of the conversation, and if someone else appears particularly interested, make a mental note to remember that individual. You might ask for a business card or write down the name later on.

As you expand your network, establish yourself as someone energetic and trustworthy. One good way to become accepted in organizations is to volunteer for the job no one wants and then perform it well. This may seem like a pointless effort if it doesn't bring you into direct contact with the kinds of people you want to meet. It pays off later, though, when you actively start looking for partners.

You may describe an excellent opportunity to an acquaintance who isn't interested or can't afford to invest but who knows someone else who can be your ideal partner. When mentioning you, the person you know can give you a good reputation simply by casual reference to the way you've conducted yourself in the past. "Yes, Joe handled the mailings for last year's fund-raiser, and he did a great job. He really knows how to get things done, and he has a lot of energy.'' Minor as it might seem, comments like that can form a good impression of you in your potential partner's mind before you ever meet.

CHECK OUT PARTNERS

When your future fortunes depend at least partly on the stability and honesty of another person, it's only good sense to learn as much as you can about that other person before entering into a relationship. We've all seen marriages turn sour, and a partnership is similar to a marriage in many ways. When it works well, a partnership, like a good marriage, enhances your life and makes everything easier; and like a bad marriage, a bad partnership brings you nothing but frustration, grief, and regrets.

You've undoubtedly heard of partnerships entered into on nothing more than a handshake and a verbal agreement. In the past that may have worked well, particularly between people who knew each other and were willing to forgive an occasional mistake. Today, however, we live in an increasingly litigious society. People sue over matters that they never would have taken to court twenty years ago, and they bring charges against people they never would have considered filing suit against in the past. Perhaps the most extreme case was the young man in Colorado who filed a multimillion-dollar lawsuit against his mother and father a few years ago, charging them with being bad parents because all their efforts failed to persuade him to finish his education. The son lost his case, but it points up the fact that these days you never know who might bring suit against you or why.

Since legal actions are so prevalent today, and because partnerships are legal contracts, your partnerships should always be based on written agreements that spell out the duties and responsibilities of each party in detail. If one or both partners will provide cash, specify exactly how much each is to contribute. If unspecified costs are to be shared, state what proportion each party will pay and any limits on either partner's contribution.

In addition to financial considerations, detail what work is to be

159

done by everyone involved, establish the schedule on which this work will be completed, and define what constitutes satisfactory performance and who will decide whether the job has been done right. Provide for arbitration in the event of a dispute, and include penalties for failure to live up to the terms, or incentives for superior performance, as these apply to the transaction. Indicate what will happen to the partnership if one of the parties is unable to continue because of illness, death, or financial or personal problems. Write in protections against illegal or irresponsible activities taken by any partner, and explain what recourse other partners will have against a partner who becomes involved in such conduct. Describe how, when, and under what conditions the partnership may be dissolved and how the assets are to be distributed at dissolution.

If you have a great deal of experience with legal documents, or feel confident that you can cover all contingencies to everyone's satisfaction, you may be able to draw up a partnership agreement on your own. However, it's really in your best interests to have an attorney at least look over what you've written. A trained lawyer will often point out possibilities you've neglected to take into consideration and can sometimes find ways the agreement could be changed slightly to offer you better protection. Most important, the attorney will tell you if you've inadvertently included something that goes against the law.

A review of an agreement you've already written may cost you whatever the attorney charges for an hour or two. If you belong to one of the legal protection plans offered by some insurance companies and department stores, you may receive several hours of free legal advice as part of the service, and this would be an excellent use of them. If you hire an attorney to prepare your agreement from scratch, the cost will depend on the lawyer's hourly rate and how complex your partnership is.

In general, the average partnership agreement should run less than $1,000 in legal fees. If you can't afford this, you might have your cash partner pay for it, repaying him later out of your share of the profits. It's a small price to pay for a service that can save you thousands of dollars and hours of legal headaches, while enabling you to enter into relationships that can make you a fortune.

160

Before signing any papers, though, be sure your potential partner is capable of performing his or her end of the deal. A financial statement checked out by your banker is good insurance. You should present similar proof of your own sincerity to the other party, even if you aren't asked for it. A formal statement of your assets and intentions demonstrates sincerity and integrity and proves you take your ventures seriously.

Remember, even when you don't have the money to purchase an investment bargain, with a little effort and ingenuity you can always find someone who does.

CHAPTER 15

Creative Uses of Other People's Money

When you see an investment you know you could profit from, but don't have the full price or an immediate buyer lined up, options and lease options are invaluable tools. These techniques allow you to tie up opportunities using a small deposit while you find the necessary financing or a buyer who will pay more than the price you negotiate. In effect, the seller's investment in the item holds it until you find a lender or buyer whose cash contribution creates your profit.

A simple option gives you the right to buy something at a predetermined price during a set time period. However, you are not required to exercise this option. You pay a small fee known as an option consideration to purchase this right. Then for as long as the option runs, the seller can sell only to you unless you waive your option. If asked to waive the option, you can charge a fee for doing so.

When you don't exercise your option—that is, purchase the item—by the time the option period runs out, you have choices. You can decide you're no longer interested and go on to something else, or you can try to negotiate an extension or new option.

To demonstrate how this might work, let's say you know someone who wants to sell a boat for $20,000. You know this boat is worth $35,000, but the owner is divorcing and is more interested in unloading the boat than in selling for top dollar. You might pay

$800 for a six-month option to buy the boat at the $20,000 price. For the next six months no one else can buy the boat, even if someone should offer the seller more money, unless you agree to waive your option. Meanwhile, you have time to find a partner or another buyer.

During your six months you might do several things, depending on your goals. If your goal is to own the boat, you might work on raising enough money to buy it outright. If you would rather make a profit, you can look for someone willing to pay $30,000 for the boat. As soon as you find your buyer, you exercise your option, buy the boat, and immediately resell.

What if, during this time, the owner should meet someone who is willing to pay $25,000 for the boat, and he asks you to waive your option? You can refuse, if you believe you'll be exercising the option. You could also agree, provided your option consideration fee is returned and you receive a little extra money for being so cooperative.

If your six-month option still has over five months to go, you could ask that your consideration fee be doubled. The closer the option is to expiring, the less money you're likely to be able to ask for waiving it, since the other parties could simply wait. It's a judgment you have to make depending on the amount of time left on your option and your knowledge of how anxious the seller and buyer are to finalize their deal.

THE LEASE OPTION

In real estate we often combine an option with a lease. This joins two separate agreements into a very advantageous contract. The lease gives you full use and control of the property just as though you owned it, except that you can't sell it outright, while the option gives you the choice of buying when your lease is up.

Many first-time home buyers use this technique to get into a house when they can't afford a large down payment. You pay an option consideration rather than a rental deposit. Some sellers will agree to apply this sum to the eventual purchase price, while others won't. Monthly payments are slightly higher than rent would be, with a portion of the rent also credited toward the final purchase. The proportion of the rent that will be applied to the purchase is negotiated between the parties, with some buyers able to get their entire payment deducted from the ultimate sale price.

Imagine that you want to buy a house that's on the market for $90,000, but you have no down payment. You could offer the seller a three-year lease option. Assuming appreciation averages 6 percent a year, the property would be worth about $107,000 at the end of your option period.

Rather than agreeing to pay full price, however, you offer a little less. Perhaps you agree to pay the present market value plus half of any additional appreciation between the date of your initial agreement and the date you exercise your option. Or you might set definite dollar values, such as $93,000 if you exercise your option after one year, $96,000 if you exercise after two years, and $100,000 at the end of three years. After all, you're taking over the house and will be guaranteeing the seller a steady monthly income, while the seller will retain tax advantages as the owner.

You pay $1,500 as an option consideration fee and get the seller to agree to credit half that toward your purchase. You might even be able to pay your consideration fee in several installments. You estimate that similar houses rent for $800 a month, so you offer to pay $950 a month rent, with $200 a month being applied to your purchase balance. At the end of three years you've accumulated a down payment of $7,950. That's more than enough to qualify you for a 95 percent FHA owner-occupant loan that you can use to purchase the house.

Investors also use lease options to control more property with less cash. There are a couple of different ways to do this, depending on your goals. One is to tie up property while you look for a buyer who will pay more than the option price you negotiated. During this time you might also fix up the house to increase its value. The other method is to use the property as a rental, charging at least enough rent to cover your monthly payments while you wait for appreciation to increase the value of the house above your agreed option price, when, again, you sell at a profit. For those who are interested in seeing what an actual lease option looks like, I've included a sample of one in the Resource Section at the end of this book (see "Cash Flow Tools").

A PROFITABLE SANDWICH

A nice variation on the lease option for investors is to do it in two directions at once, which is known as a "sandwich" lease option. As the investor, you negotiate a good price and the longest terms you can on a lease option. Then you turn around and lease option to another party, your lease-option tenant. Set your tenant's monthly payments at least equal to what you've agreed to pay the owner, or a little more, and the tenant's purchase price high enough to allow you a profit.

Most important, allow your tenants a shorter option period—a year less than your option period with the owner. The year's difference between the tenant's option and your own gives you a nice safety margin. If anything should prevent your tenants from per-

---

$$ MONEYMAKER $$

Marty took a six-month lease option on a house in a high-priced California suburb. He paid $1,500 consideration and negotiated a monthly rent of $1,000 and a final purchase price of $135,000. He also agreed to make a down payment of $14,000 when he exercised his option.

For a few hundred dollars Marty painted the house and installed new carpets, improving the appearance so much that the owners wanted it back. However, they could not go back on their legal contract with Marty. He started showing the house before even exercising his option, and several potential buyers expressed interest.

Having no money to make the $14,000 down payment when he exercised his option, Marty located a friend of a friend who made him a short-term loan that allowed him to make the down payment. He bought the house on the eighth of the month for $135,000 and sold it on the twenty-fifth for $205,500. After paying back the $14,000 loan and deducting his closing costs, consideration, and "fixer" expenses, Marty made over $50,000 profit on that one house.

---

forming on their option, you have time to arrange for another buyer or for financing if you decide to buy the house yourself.

When your tenants exercise their option with you to buy the property, you turn around and exercise your option with the owner. You buy the property and immediately sign it over to your tenants, then pocket the difference in the two prices.

Yes, this is legal. The beauty of it is, it costs you nothing. You pay a consideration for a lease option and then charge your tenants a slightly higher consideration. The tenants cover the monthly rent and perhaps a bit more. The tenants also take care of all maintenance on the property, since they're the eventual owners. Then when they exercise their option, you pocket several thousand dollars.

The worst that can happen is that your tenants don't exercise their option and you can neither find another buyer nor line up financing. If that should ever happen, you simply decline to exercise your option and have lost nothing.

Two points to keep in mind with lease options: 1) *Always* make sure your option against a property is recorded against the title. 2) When using sandwich lease options, your contract with the owner must *include* the right to sublet, while your contract with your tenants should specifically *prohibit* sublets. This allows you complete control over the property.

EQUITY SHARING

Consider this: Nationwide, no more than 60 percent of the population can afford to purchase a median-priced home. In high-cost areas, as much as 80 percent of potential home buyers are locked out of the market. Yet demand for single-family housing is still high.

Now look at this situation as an investor. You can make money for yourself and, while doing so, perform a tremendous service to people who want to buy a home but can't afford it. The answer lies in combining lease options and equity sharing (a term that will be explained in a moment).

It's often hard to purchase a property with a lot of leverage and still have a positive cash flow. You don't want large negative cash flows on several properties. Equity sharing can be one method to

167

guarantee positive cash flow, enabling you to move on and buy more property. It also enables you to hold on to a property if you don't want to sell it just yet. After all, the longer you hold ownership to a good property, the more money you'll make.

To eliminate a negative cash flow, why not sell half interest in a property to a partner? Your partner will live in the house and make the monthly payments. If you can acquire good properties with maximum leverage and structure the monthly payments so you can sell half ownership and have your partner make the payments, you've got a winner. You can hold on to at least half ownership in many properties, not just one, and yet not have to lie awake nights worrying about cash flow.

How Equity Sharing Works

There are three ways to structure an equity-sharing deal, plus infinite variations within each way, depending on the specifics of your situation. Once you have a property and potential partner in mind, you'll need to decide whether to set up your purchase as a straight equity share, a lease option, or a combined lease option and equity share.

Equity sharing is a form of partnership for the purpose of owning real estate. The individuals involved in the partnership generally take title to the real estate as tenants in common, each having an undivided interest without the right of survivorship (they don't inherit each other's share).

$$ MONEYMAKER $$

Alan had some money to invest and his friend Dan was a skilled carpenter. They bought a house in need of extensive repairs together on an equity-sharing agreement in which Alan handled the financing and Dan took care of the rehabilitation. After paying an initial $25,000, they put the house into tip-top condition for a cost of approximately $11,000 in materials and the carpenter's labor. They then sold the property for $60,000 and made tidy profits of $12,000 each.

The most common way the partnership works is for an investor and a home partner to purchase a house together. The investor supplies the down payment, and the home partner lives in the house and makes the monthly payments. They divide the ownership fifty-fifty and share equally in the appreciation when the house is sold or when one partner buys out the other.

The investor can be either a seller who retains some of his equity in a property or someone who puts up the cash for a down payment. The home partner is expected not only to make the mortgage payments, but to pay the property taxes and insurance and take care of the routine maintenance of the property.

I've given you this example to help you understand the concept, but I cannot stress enough that there is no one "standard" or "right" way to structure an equity-sharing arrangement. It all depends on what works best for the individuals involved. The percentage of ownership can be different: ten-ninety, forty-sixty, one-third–two-thirds, for example. The investor may help with the monthly payments, or the home partner may pay part of the down payment. The Resource Section at the end of this book contains a sample equity-sharing contract, but remember that this is only one way of many that these deals can be structured.

Since you're sharing title to the house from the start in equity sharing, you should choose your partner carefully. I would feel most comfortable using a straight equity-sharing contract if

- I knew the partner well
- He or she had flawless credit and stability, and
- I didn't have much equity in the house

SELLING ON LEASE OPTION

When you sell property you own on a lease option, you continue to own the home—your name is the only one on the title. You're giving your partner a lease with an option to purchase at the end of the lease period. He pays an option consideration for the option.

Just as when you buy on a lease option, if the tenant/partner exercises the option, a set portion of his rent payments is credited toward the purchase price. In addition, he's given credit for one-half of the appreciation in value between the time the agreement was signed and the time he exercises the option. This way the partner builds up some equity in the property while leasing, provided he actually purchases the property at the end.

What advantage does this have for the investor? First, you can charge a higher lease payment than you could get for a month-to-month rental, thereby eliminating any negative cash flow. After all, part of it is going toward the eventual purchase. If the partner doesn't buy the house, you get to keep the amount that would have been credited toward the purchase. You don't have to refund it.

Second, you have many of the advantages of an equity-sharing arrangement but keep the title in your name. One difficulty of other forms of partnership is getting the partner off the title if he or she defaults. With a lease option you don't have to worry about that.

Third, you most likely have a buyer at the end of the lease-option period, and you'll get the price agreed on beforehand or fair market value according to an appraisal if you can't agree on a price.

You would want to use this method if you have a potential partner who doesn't seem very committed to the property or if you are not confident that he can meet his obligations. This way, if he defaults, you can terminate the lease and it becomes a month-to-month rental, subject to eviction. If the partner is serious about the house and makes his payments as he should, however, he does well in the long run.

COMBINE LEASE OPTIONS WITH EQUITY SHARING

In my view, this is the best way to use equity sharing. Over the years, through experience, I have found this the most risk-free way to structure an agreement. A sample contract for this type of agreement can be found in the Resource Section at the end of this book (see "Cash Flow Tools").

At first the agreement functions as a lease option. At the end of the option period, if the partner exercises the option, it converts to an equity-sharing agreement and the partner's name goes on the title as co-owner.

What this says to your partner is: I'll lease my house to you for a set period. At the end of that period, you have the option to own part of the property and be put on the title under certain conditions. These conditions include making all the payments on time, taking care of the premises, and being an all-around good guy. The lease period gives you time to be sure your partner is responsible and will meet his obligations. It gives him the chance to be sure he really wants the house and is willing and able to do what it takes to obtain co-ownership.

The lease-option period can be whatever you wish—six months if you don't have any doubts about your partner or as long as five years. If you do run into a problem during the lease period, as before, you can terminate the lease and evict your would-be partner, and he loses his option. The responsible home partner doesn't lose out with this type of agreement, either. He's building up equity and appreciation during the lease period and at the end has the same degree of co-ownership as if you started out with a straight equity-sharing agreement.

I like to have as much control as I can over my properties, and this is the way to do it while still providing the home partner with benefits, too. After all, you come out of it with your investment protected, while he comes out of it with a home to live in and equity built up to help him realize the American dream of home ownership.

Professional real estate investors used to say that equity sharing worked best when interest rates were high or the real estate market was slow. It's still true that it really shines in those times or when you may have a negative cash flow if you complete a standard purchase. But in this age of high housing prices, with so many people being forced to rent, equity sharing can work in all times and all markets.

THE BASIC ADVANTAGES OF EQUITY SHARING

FOR THE INVESTOR

- Provides positive cash flow for highly leveraged investments
- May help qualify for new financing with home partner
- Retains a portion of the ownership as a tenant in common
- Has tax benefits, including depreciation
- Receives a portion of all future appreciation

FOR THE HOME PARTNER

- Enjoys the use of the home and builds up equity in it
- Easier to qualify for a loan, if necessary
- Acquires a portion of the ownership as a tenant in common
- Has tax benefits as a homeowner
- Receives a portion of all future appreciation

THE AGREEMENT

The backbone of the equity-sharing arrangement is the agreement. This should be a formal contract drawn by a capable attorney and should clearly indicate the responsibilities of both the investor and home partner.

A contract can be adapted to a multitude of individual situations for both investor and home partner. Since there's so much variation in each transaction, an attorney is a must.

You'll save yourself headaches later on if you make certain that both you and your partner understand clearly all the details of the contract (which can get lost in the legal jargon) and that you are in agreement on exactly how this is going to work. If you find that you don't agree, you can sit down together and straighten it out before you sign the agreement.

The various forms of lease options and equity sharing are creative ways to buy, hold, or resell a property with a minimum investment when you purchase, a positive cash flow while you own, and a nice profit when you sell.

172

CHAPTER **16**

Paper Profits You Can Spend

Once you begin to accumulate assets, you can start doing some really creative things. The profit spiral becomes more and more powerful as you multiply your holdings. This is particularly true in real estate, the area in which I believe these arrangements work the best.

When you own something that has value, you can borrow against it. Profits from sales are taxed, while money borrowed as loans against assets is not. Therefore, taking out loans gives you tax-free cash that you can spend as you like. Naturally, in the early stages of your investment plan I recommend you only use this cash to make more investments so that you can pay back your loans out of profits.

With real estate, you can normally borrow up to 80 percent of the value of your property with very little trouble and can often borrow as much as 90 percent. Sometimes, though, conventional lenders such as banks or savings and loans don't give us the terms we'd like. The interest or payment rates may be so high that we would have trouble structuring a profit into any deal we finance with the loan.

WRITING YOUR OWN LOANS

Happily for us as investors, we don't have to live with whatever the banks choose to give us. We can write our own loans against our properties. Stationery and business supply houses or title companies can furnish us with standard loan forms on which the payment schedules and interest rates are left blank, or we can copy the wording from another loan paper. Then we simply fill in terms that will work for us.

There are certain limits on this, of course. We can't write loans for more than the property is worth, and we have to stay within the range of what the marketplace will accept. However, the marketplace is often far more flexible than bankers' guidelines.

When you write your own loans, or notes, it's called "creating paper." Once you've created paper against your property, you have two choices: you can sell the paper to an investor who will give you immediate cash for your note in return for collecting the payments plus interest for future profit; or you can use the paper itself like money to pay for something you buy.

Of these two approaches, I prefer the second. When you sell paper to an investor, you usually have to discount it. For example, say you create a $40,000 note at 9 percent simple interest, payable interest only at yearly intervals for five years, when the $40,000 principal comes due in one balloon payment. This means whoever buys your note receives only $3,600 once a year until the note falls due five years in the future. An investor who considers buying this note is likely to think that's not a very good return on $40,000. He or she can probably do better investing in a money market fund.

However, the investor might be interested in buying your note for $30,000. You get the $30,000 cash immediately but pay back 9 percent interest on $40,000 annually and then pay off the loan principal at the end of five years with one $40,000 payment. For a $30,000 investment the investor receives $3,600 a year, which is a 12 percent annual return on $30,000, and then makes an additional $10,000 profit when you pay off the $40,000 loan.

When you need $30,000 and want to keep your payments low, this might be a good deal, especially if you use the money to buy into an extremely profitable investment. A better deal, though, could be to use your note directly as a $40,000 partial payment on whatever you're buying. A seller who wants to get rid of a house in a hurry and doesn't need all the cash right away might consider this as money in the bank.

In fact, someone I know once created a note very similar to this to buy a house. The seller had a new job halfway across the country and was moving from a high-priced housing market to a lower-priced market, so he didn't need all the cash from the sale of his home right away. The seller also had a thirteen-year-old daughter who would be starting college in five years. In addition to paying annual interest of $3,200, the buyer arranged for the note to start paying off the principal, beginning in five years, at $10,000 every year for four years. As far as the seller was concerned, that note was his little girl's college fund, and everyone walked away smiling.

Whenever you buy anything from a private party, you can offer a note against real estate you own. For instance, say you have a rental property earning positive cash flow. Write a note against it, use the note to buy a boat, and let the rent pay off your cabin cruiser. You don't have to pay loan fees to a bank, and you can arrange whatever terms you can negotiate with the person selling the boat.

━━━━ $$ MONEYMAKER $$ ━━━━

Joe couldn't afford the down payment on a house in the high-priced area near his job. He went to a small but rapidly growing town seventy-five miles away and found a seller facing foreclosure. For $2,000 cash Joe assumed the seller's $50,000 FHA loan on a house worth $65,000.

Two years later the house was worth $75,000. Joe created a $15,000 note against the property at 10 percent interest, paying interest only on monthly terms for three years. Using this note as a down payment, Joe bought a house for $120,000 near his job. The seller carried back another $10,000 at 11 percent for three years, compounded annually, with no payments until the end of the term.

Joe rented out his first house, and the rent he received covered that house's payments and the interest payments on the note he had created against it. When the notes against both his houses came due three years later, Joe sold the rental house for $90,000, paid off both notes and the agent's commission, and pocketed $5,000—and now he owned his own home near his workplace.

BUYING PAPER TO SPEND

When you have some cash to invest, you can work the note market from the other end. As we discussed earlier, investors buy notes at discounts. Loan brokers in most cities handle these transactions, or you can buy for yourself. If you check out the ads in your newspaper, you'll probably see a few that say something like "Cash for Your Notes" or "I Buy Real Estate Loans." Many of these are placed by independent investors.

You can run your own ad. Some of those who respond will be investors trying to sell paper they've created. Others will be people who have sold property and agreed to carry part of the financing, but who then want cash before the note falls due.

When you first get into this market, you'll have to move carefully until you learn the ropes. I recommend you make your first few purchases through a loan broker who can advise you about the relative worth of various notes.

When you're the buyer, you want to negotiate a good discount for yourself. For instance, if someone offers you a note with a face value of $25,000, you don't pay out that much. Look carefully at the terms, the value of the property the note is written against, and the record of the person who is supposed to pay you. In general, the less attractive the terms, the bigger the discount.

Shopping the Paper Market

New loans, those on which few or no payments have been made, are usually the least valuable. They haven't established a track record. When a solid payment record has accumulated, the note is said to be "seasoned" and is worth more.

High interest rates, short loan periods, loans that pay compound rather than simple interest, loans with frequent payments, and loans that pay off part of the principal as well as the interest are worth more. Low interest rates, long payback periods, simple interest, infrequent payments, and loans that pay interest only or less than interest are worth less. Basically, any note that returns more money in a shorter time with lower risk sells for closer to face value.

176

In addition to profit considerations, you'll also want to check how secure the note is. Be sure any note you buy is recorded against the property's title, and look for its position and the total amount of loans compared to the property's value. If it's a second mortgage or trust deed and total loans against the property add up to 85 percent of value or less, that's usually a fairly safe position.

Notes in third position are considered a little more risky, and fourth loans may be dangerous. Although it's not unheard of to see loans in fifth, sixth, seventh, or even lower positions, I'd look very carefully at the property's total value before buying any of these. If the property still has plenty of equity, maybe it's all right, but I'd wonder why the borrower didn't simply refinance or at least take out one big second loan to pay off all the lower-position notes. The person could be sliding into deep financial waters and has been taking out new loans to keep up with payments on the old ones. If that's the case, you might be able to make a good deal to buy the property before the seller's situation gets any worse.

Strong and Weak Notes

Let's look again at the example of the $25,000 note. You might find that it's in second position and the house is only mortgaged for 75 percent of value. The note is two years old, pays 13 percent compound interest, and monthly payments are amortized to pay off in full in three years' time. The borrower has made every payment a few days early and has made a couple of extra payments. This is a strong note and won't discount for as much as a weaker note would. You might get it for around $20,000, but the seller could expect more—perhaps as much as $22,000 or $23,000.

By way of contrast, compare this with a $25,000 fourth note that's only six months old on a house that's mortgaged for 95 percent of value. Simple interest is 9.5 percent, and interest only is paid quarterly with the full principal due in one payment seven years from now. The borrower has made the only two payments due so far, but the second one was five days late. This is an extremely weak note; personally I'd rather pass on it altogether and look for something more promising. If you think the property is due to appreciate rapidly and feel like gambling, you might offer $10,000 for it.

When you buy a note against real estate, you have a lien against the property. That's your security against default, and if payments aren't made according to the written terms, you can foreclose. You should send notices to any lenders in higher positions to notify you if the borrower gets behind in payments to them.

HIGH AND LOW NOTE DISCOUNT FACTORS

HIGH DISCOUNT	LOW DISCOUNT
• Unseasoned—fairly new note, short payment record	• Seasoned—note has existed long enough to establish solid payment record
• Low position—fourth, fifth, or lower lien	• High position—first, second, or third lien
• Weak equity—loans for more than 90 percent of market value against property	• Strong equity—loans for 85 percent or less of market value against property
• Low interest rate	• High interest rate
• Long payback period	• Short payback period
• Simple interest	• Compound interest
• Infrequent payments—quarterly or fewer	• Frequent payments—monthly or every two months
• Interest only or less than interest only payments	• Pays interest plus some principal
• Borrower has poor credit	• Borrower has good credit

USES FOR DISCOUNTED NOTES

Buying discounted notes is a good way to increase your cash flow. If you paid $30,000 for the $40,000 note we spoke of earlier, you could be the one collecting 12 percent on your money until the $40,000 final payment paid you a $10,000 profit. Over the five years you'd make $58,000 on your $30,000 investment, which is a pretty good return for doing nothing but cashing checks.

You can make the same investments with notes you buy that you would with paper you create yourself, only for less money. If you

178

$$ MONEYMAKER $$

When Tony's marriage failed, he felt terrible; he felt even worse when he saw the property settlement. His wife asked for half their assets. As it happened, their only assets were $38,000 in cash and Tony's beloved $50,000 BMW, and the lawyers said Tony had to sell the car so everything could be divided evenly.

Happily for Tony, his brother Pete had the solution. He took Tony's cash and bought a selection of discounted real estate notes with total face values of $50,000. The wife was happy to accept the income-producing notes as her share of the settlement, while Tony sighed with relief as he and the BMW tooled off into the sunset together.

---

bought that $40,000 note for $30,000, you could turn around and use it as a payment against something you buy. The person who accepted it might ask for a discount, too, but you'd negotiate that in your favor. Instead of $40,000, you might be credited with $35,000. On the other hand, the other party might just accept it at full value.

You can also use discounted notes as gifts. You might give one to your parents for some extra income or place a few in trusts to accumulate value for your children. Donate one to your college, your church, or your favorite charity. The recipients benefit from larger sums than if you simply provided the amount of cash you spent for the notes.

Once you discover the wonderful world of notes, you may decide never to work again. After all, you could simply let your money go on making money for you while you relax on a tropical beach, ski every mountain in Europe, or do whatever you prefer.

CHAPTER **17**

Smiling All the Way to the Bank

Did you ever see one of those movies about making movies? There's always a scene where the actors gather on the set in their costumes. Assistants run around adjusting garments and touching up makeup. Then the director yells, "Lights . . . camera . . . action!" and everyone goes into their rehearsed moves and speaks the lines that were written for them.

Sometimes it would be nice if life were more like the movies. We would accept only the roles that let us be rich and beautiful, and we'd always have a happy ending. Best of all, the only effort we'd have to make would be to get out of bed and climb into the studio limousine. There'd always be someone around to tell us exactly what to do and say and when to go into action.

The lives most of us lead aren't like that, and even if you're an actor who works steadily, your real, personal life doesn't go that way, either. No one can give us the magic words that will bring us guaranteed success, and there isn't anyone to tell us how and when to act.

Instead we have something that's a lot more interesting and more fun. We get to decide for ourselves what we're going to do and when we're going to do it. The trouble is, a lot of people don't understand that. They spend their entire lives waiting for someone else to come along and tell them how to be successful. If you've fallen into the habit of waiting for someone to direct you, I'll do it right now. Your time for success has arrived. This is it. I hope you're ready. Action!

"Hey, wait!" I can hear you saying. "What are my lines? Where do I stand? What do I do next? And after that, and after that?"

To push this dramatic metaphor just a little further, even though Shakespeare wrote that all the world's a stage, in my opinion real life is like improvisational theater. You have a general idea of your own situation, your motivation, and what you want to achieve. But it's up to you to write your own lines and take your own actions. You have to play off other characters; some of them will help you, while others may try to upstage you. If you don't play your part well enough, you may be replaced, but you can always audition for another production. And the more experience you get, the better your opportunity to become a star.

To get back to real-world terms, I can give you guidelines, make suggestions, and advise you on the best way to meet your goals. But neither I nor anyone else can tell you exactly what to do and say every minute of your working life to guarantee you get everything you desire. You have to figure out those things as you go along.

YOU ARE IN CHARGE

After all, only you know exactly what your goals are and what abilities and talents you bring to your work. You're the only one who understands the opportunities and problems you face every day. By the same token, you're the only one who can decide which opportunities you'll pursue or pass up and how you'll cope with your problems.

Remember my formula for financial independence:

$$Plan + Discipline = Success$$

When you design your own plan, the only limit on the success you reach is the amount of discipline you exercise over yourself. It's truly up to you. In my own life and in the lives of my students, I've seen the proof that anyone who truly desires to change his or her life and who works at it consistently can achieve far more than most people settle for. You never have to accept less than what you want unless you give up on yourself. And aren't you worth that extra effort to turn your dreams of financial independence into reality?

Sure, sometimes you'll become tired or discouraged. Everyone does. That's why I advise all my students, and that includes you, to build some fun and relaxation into their lives. You're not a machine, you're a human being. Schedule time for activities you enjoy, and take care of yourself. You won't enjoy reaching your goals if you wear yourself out getting there.

Spend some leisure time with the special people in your life, and explain what you're doing and why. Let them know you're working now so that all of you can enjoy a better future. Take them along to some auctions or to look at properties you plan to buy so they can share the fun and excitement, and celebrate with them when you complete a step toward your goal.

TAKE A FREE VACATION

One way to celebrate, and to reward yourself and those you care about, is to take a vacation. Better yet, how would you like to spend next February lolling on a Jamaican beach or touring New Zealand—for free? Opportunities like that are available when you know where to find them.

It's not that difficult to line up free travel, including cruises, airfare to most parts of the world, hotel rooms, and sometimes even meals. You work with a travel agent to choose the trip or tour you want, then make reservations for a group tour. Numbers vary, but in general, for signing up approximately fifteen travelers, one person receives a free ticket. Find other people who want to take the same trip you do. Get them to commit and pay in advance, and you travel for nothing.

You don't have to be a high roller with lots of rich friends to make this work. I recently heard of some city employees who did it. One employee organized a low-cost Caribbean cruise and offered it to everyone else who worked for the city. Secretaries, park and street maintenance workers, water plant operators, and bookkeepers signed on. Everyone had a great time, at reasonable cost—and the organizer took a complimentary cruise.

You could try this where you work or through your church, professional organization, or hobby groups. Many people save all year to take special vacations, and when you present them with one that's already arranged to take advantage of good rates in attractive locations, they're happy to join you. Another plus for many is the opportunity to travel with people they know.

The kinds of trips you can offer depend partly on what's available through local travel agencies and partly on what terms you can negotiate. Some agents don't like to share these free tickets, because they use them for their own travels or as employee bonuses. If you run into one of those, call a rival agency, even one in another town.

In January 1989 a quick survey of travel agents in my area turned up a week in Jamaica that included air travel, hotel, three buffet meals a day, and drinks, all for a price of $2,400 for two people. Another package tour, this one to New Zealand, offered round-trip airfare and hotel at $945 per person. Anyone who could enroll fifteen or more for either of these trips would receive a free ticket. The New Zealand vacation also included a half-price discount for signing up between ten and fifteen people.

Travel agents advise you to book early, since the lowest-cost trips fill up before the others. Also, signing up several months in advance locks in low prices in case costs go up, so plan ahead to get the best deals. Eight months to a year in advance gives you enough lead time in most cases. This also allows plenty of time to sign up the number of people you need to fill your tour. Remember, some businesses set up their vacation calendars in January, so folks need time to arrange their holiday schedules and save up their fares.

When booking cruises or resort stays, take into account the people who are likely to sign up with you. Some ships and hotels cater to a young crowd that likes to boogie all night, while others appeal to an older, more sedate group. Your travel agent is your best adviser here.

Success depends on finding the right agency and destination, negotiating good terms, and then signing up enough people to fill your quota. It's a simple way to give yourself a free dream vacation.

━━━━━━ $$ MONEYMAKER $$ ━━━━━━

Every citizen who travels outside the United States is allowed to bring home a certain amount of foreign merchandise without paying customs duty; as of this writing the limit is $400 worth. You might travel to a country such as Spain, where you could buy something like hand-tooled leather purses for $10 apiece. If you were to buy forty purses and bring them home, duty free, you could easily sell those purses to friends and neighbors for at least $50 each.

With a $40 profit on each of forty purses, your gain would be $1,600. If you've negotiated your ticket prices well, that should come close to covering the cost of taking another person along on your trip—another person who could also bring home $400 worth of duty-free merchandise.

BRING YOUR DREAMS BACK TO EARTH

While you're dreaming about your vacation, let your imagination throw out some other things you'd like to include in your life. Don't worry about whether these ideas are practical or obtainable. They're your dreams, and they can be anything you choose. If they excite you or make you laugh out loud, great.

Then write them all down, every crazy whim, the small ones and the big ones—the bigger the better. When you're done, you'll have a list of goals. That's right. These are the things you really want, and they're the reasons you desire financial independence. Investments and deals that bring in the money you need to realize these dreams are only the tools to reach your goals.

Once you realize that, investing takes on new meaning. Every auction bargain is a step closer to the Austrian ski slopes; every successful real estate deal is another payment on your personal jet; each lease option is another semester at Harvard Medical School for your pride and joy.

When you see your investment program in terms of how it turns dreams into realities, life becomes exciting. You look forward to every day and every challenge with enthusiasm. That's when you step into the spotlight and take center stage, ready to make nothing but money.

185

CHAPTER **18**

Your Most Important Step

I've tried to give you all the information you need to start up the profit spiral and reach your financial goals, whatever they may be. The techniques and ideas in this book can help you buy your first home and take you all the way to millionaire status. Now it's up to you. You have the system; but you must set your goals and devise your own plan, then apply the discipline to turn your dreams into reality. No one else can do that for you. But if you determine to make use of the knowledge you now have, you can change your life in any way you want.

With that in mind, review all the different ideas I've offered you. Work on developing the ten characteristics of successful people described in chapter 2, and choose the first step that will start you on your way. Once you've accomplished that, take another step and then another, and never stop until you reach your goal.

Study the chapters in this book that interest you most, and take advantage of the suggestions for sources where you can learn more. Study the final two chapters for information on where to find bargain properties and how to structure lease-option and equity-sharing deals. Make contacts and ask questions. Ask for partners, ask for deals, ask for more money. You may not always get everything you ask for; but if you don't ask, you'll never get anything.

$$ MONEYMAKER $$

Would you like to earn an extra income every year? The current median wage is just under $15,000 a year. Earning an extra $15,000 a year part-time while holding down a job takes a system and some discipline, but it can be done. Proper use of time is essential; you can't waste it watching the average person's seven hours of television a day and playing every weekend. Instead, study distress property purchasing techniques in the evenings and have a real estate agent look for your properties while you're at your job. On weekends inspect the properties your agent has found. All you need is one good deal to make you as much as many people—perhaps even you—earn in an entire year.

Call my office and ask for a free copy of my newsletter, Dave Del Dotto's *Cash Flow Report,* and ask my hotline advisers for more information. Telephone 1-800-554-3000 or write to us at

Del Dotto Enterprises
1500 J Street
Modesto, California 95354

In fact, even if you don't need extra help, contact us anyway. I'm always happy to hear from my readers and students. If you make any particularly good deals, you could end up as one of the success stories featured in my newsletter or interviewed on my television show. Nothing would make me happier than to hear that every person who reads this book has gone on to make nothing but money.

PART IV

Wealth Resources

Bargain Hunter's Guide

The following listings show offices of the federal agencies that offer the best opportunities for auction bargains and good real estate buys in the leading cities of each state and the District of Columbia. If you live or are buying property some distance from a large city and have difficulty locating the nearest office of the agency you want, contact the office listed here that's closest to the area you're interested in. They'll be able to tell you about any offices closer to where you want to buy.

MONTGOMERY, ALABAMA

> HUD/FHA
> 474 S. Court St.
> Montgomery, AL 36104
>
> Veterans Administration
> 474 S. Court St.
> Montgomery, AL 36104
>
> U.S. Marshal's Office
> U.S. Courthouse
> Property/Civil/Evidence Section
> P.O. Drawer 4249
> Montgomery, AL 36103
> There is no mailing list for this agency. Check local newspaper under
>   "Legal Notices."

U.S. Bankruptcy Court
Middle Alabama/One Court Square
Montgomery, AL 36104
Check local paper for sales.

ANCHORAGE, ALASKA

HUD/FHA
701 C St.
Anchorage, AK 99513

Farmers Home Administration
634 S. Bailey, Su. 103
Palmer, AK 99645

Veterans Administration
235 E. 8th Ave.
Anchorage, AK 99501

U.S. Marshal's Office
Property/Civil/Evidence Section
Department of Justice
701 C St.
Anchorage, AK 99513
No list. Check local papers for sale notices.

U.S. Bankruptcy Court
701 C St.
Anchorage, AK 99501

PHOENIX, ARIZONA

HUD/FHA
101 N. 1st St.
Phoenix, AZ 85004-2360

Farmers Home Administration
201 E. Indianola, Su. 275
Phoenix, AZ 85012
Properties auctioned.

Veterans Administration
3225 N. Central Ave.
Phoenix, AZ 85012

U.S. Marshal's Office
Property/Civil/Evidence Section
230 N. 1st Ave.
Phoenix, AZ 85025
Sales are advertised in local papers by auctioneer.

U.S. Bankruptcy Court
230 N. 1st Ave.
Phoenix, AZ 85025

LITTLE ROCK, ARKANSAS

HUD/FHA
523 Louisiana St., Su. 200
Little Rock, AR 77201-3707

Farmers Home Administration
Arkansas State Office
700 West Capitol
Little Rock, AR 72201

Veterans Administration
1200 W. 3rd
Little Rock, AR 72201

U.S. Marshal's Office
Property/Civil/Evidence Section
600 W. Capitol
Little Rock, AR 72201

U.S. Bankruptcy Court
Post Office Bldg., Rm. 445
Little Rock, AR 72201
No list. Check local papers for sale notices.

LOS ANGELES, CALIFORNIA

HUD/FHA
2500 Wilshire Blvd.
Los Angeles, CA 90057

Veterans Administration
11000 Wilshire Blvd.
Los Angeles, CA 90024

U.S. Marshal's Office
Property/Civil/Evidence Section
U.S. Department of Justice
312 N. Spring
Los Angeles, CA 90012

U.S. Bankruptcy Court
312 N. Spring
Los Angeles, CA 90012

SAN FRANCISCO, CALIFORNIA

HUD/FHA
450 Golden Gate Ave.
P.O. Box 36003
San Francisco, CA 94102

Veterans Administration
211 Main St.
San Francisco, CA 94105

U.S. Marshal's Office
Property/Civil/Evidence Section
450 Golden Gate Ave.
P.O. Box 36056
San Francisco, CA 94102

U.S. Bankruptcy Court
450 Golden Gate Ave.
San Francisco, CA 94102
No mailing list. Contact individual trustees.

DENVER, COLORADO

HUD/FHA
Property Disposition Division
Foreclosed houses are listed in local newspapers on Saturday and
    Sunday. See property with Realtor of your choice and have him fill
    out bid on properties of interest. Then submit bid to HUD.

Farmers Home Administration
U.S. Dept. of Agriculture
2490 West 26th Ave., Rm. 231
Denver, CO 80211

Veterans Administration
P.O. Box 25126
Denver, CO 80225

U.S. Marshal's Office
Property/Civil/Evidence Section
National Asset & Seizure Program
Federal Bldg., Rm. 465
1961 Stout St.
Denver, CO 80294

U.S. Bankruptcy Court
1845 Sherman
Denver, CO 80203

HARTFORD, CONNECTICUT

HUD/FHA
1 Hartford Square West
Hartford, CT 06106

Farmers Home Administration
County Office
340 Broad Windsor
Windsor, CT 06095

Veterans Administration
Regional Office
450 Main
Hartford, CT 06103

U.S. Marshal's Office
Property/Civil/Evidence Section
450 Main
Hartford, CT 06103

U.S. Bankruptcy Court
450 Main
Hartford, CT 06103

DOVER, DELAWARE

HUD/FHA
105 S. Seventh St.
Philadelphia, PA 19106

Veterans Administration
P.O. Box 8079
Philadelphia, PA 19101

U.S. Marshal's Office
844 King St.
Wilmington, DE 19801

U.S. Bankruptcy Court
Federal Building—Lock Box 38
844 King St.
Wilmington, DE 19801

DISTRICT OF COLUMBIA

HUD/FHA
1875 Connecticut Ave. N.W.
Washington, D.C. 20009

Veterans Administration
810 Vermont Ave., N.W.
Washington, D.C. 20420

U.S. Marshal's Office
Property/Civil/Evidence Section
Constitution Ave., John Marshall Pl. N.W.
Washington, D.C. 20001
Advertises in *The Washington Post.*

U.S. Bankruptcy Court
Room 1130, U.S. Courthouse
Washington, D.C. 20001

MIAMI, FLORIDA

HUD/FHA
1320 South Dixie Highway
Coral Gables, FL 33146

Farmers Home Administration
381 Krome Avenue
Homestead, FL 33031

196

Veterans Administration
Federal Bldg., Rm. 100
51 SW 1st Ave.
Miami, FL 33130

U.S. Bankruptcy Court
51 SW 1st Ave.
Miami, FL 33130

TAMPA, FLORIDA

HUD/FHA
P.O. Box 2097
Tampa, FL 33601

Veterans Administration
P.O. Box 1437
St. Petersburg, FL 33731

U.S. Marshal's Office
Property/Civil/Evidence Section
611 North Florida Ave.
Tampa, FL 33602
No mailing list. Check local newspaper.

U.S. Bankruptcy Court
700 Twiggs, Rm. 708
Tampa, FL 33602
No mailing list. Sales are posted in book in lobby.
Handled by
U.S. Trustees Office
4921 Memorial Hwy., Su. 340
Tampa, FL 33634

ATLANTA, GEORGIA

HUD/FHA
Richard B. Russell Bldg.
75 Spring St. S.W.
Atlanta, GA 30303

Farmers Home Administration
P.O. Box 326
Atlanta, GA 30253

Veterans Administration
730 Peachtree St. N.E.
Atlanta, GA 30365

U.S. Marshal's Office
Property/Civil/Evidence Section
Richard B. Russell Bldg.
75 Spring St. S.W., Rm. 1669
Atlanta, GA 30303
Auctions held first Tuesday of the month. Published in the *Atlanta Journal-Constitution*.

U.S. Bankruptcy Court
R. B. Ruther Bldg.
75 Spring St. S.W., Rm. 1340
Atlanta, GA 30303

HONOLULU, HAWAII

HUD/FHA
300 Ala Moana Blvd.
P.O. Box 50007
Honolulu, HI 96850-4991
Advertises in Sunday's *Honolulu Star Bulletin*.

Farmers Home Administration
P.O. Box 50224
Honolulu, HI 96850

Veterans Administration
P.O. Box 50188
Honolulu, HI 96850

U.S. Marshal's Office
Property/Civil/Evidence Division
Prince Kuhio Federal Bldg.
300 Ala Moana Blvd.
Honolulu, HI 96850
or
P.O. Box 50184
Sales are advertised in the *Honolulu Star Bulletin* and the *Honolulu Star Advertiser*.

198

U.S. Bankruptcy Court
Bankruptcy Clerk's Office
Prince Kuhio Federal Bldg.
P.O. Box 50121
Honolulu, HI 96850

BOISE, IDAHO

HUD/FHA
550 West Fort
Boise, ID 83702

Farmers Home Administration
870 North Linder
Meridian, ID 83642

Veterans Administration
550 West Fort
Boise, ID 83702

U.S. Marshal's Office
550 West Fort
Boise, ID 83702
Attn: Property Section

U.S. Bankruptcy Court
P.O. Box 2600
Boise, ID 83702

CHICAGO, ILLINOIS

HUD/FHA
1 N. Dearborn
Chicago, IL 60602

Veterans Administration
536 South Clark
Chicago, IL 60605

U.S. Marshal's Office
Property/Civil/Evidence Section
U.S. Marshal's Service
2195 Dearborn
Chicago, IL 60616

U.S. Bankruptcy Court
219 Dearborn St.
Chicago, IL 60604

INDIANAPOLIS, INDIANA

HUD/FHA
151 North Delaware, Rm. 350
Indianapolis, IN 46204

Farmers Home Administration
5610 Crawfordsville Road, Su. 1700
Indianapolis, IN 46224

Veterans Administration
575 North Pennsylvania
Indianapolis, IN 46204

U.S. Marshal's Office
Property/Civil/Evidence Section
46 East Ohio
Indianapolis, IN 46204
They request that you do not call to find out about the auctions. They
   handle over sixty counties. Please check the local newspapers for
   sale notices. No overall list.

U.S. Customs Service (Personal Property)
Port Director's Office
P.O. Box 51612
Indianapolis, IN 46251-0612
Can get on mailing list.

U.S. Bankruptcy Court
Courthouse, Rm. 123
46 East Ohio St.
Indianapolis, IN 46204

DES MOINES, IOWA

HUD/FHA
210 Walnut St.
Des Moines, IA 50309

Farmers Home Administration
210 Walnut St.
Des Moines, IA 50309

Veterans Administration
210 Walnut St.
Des Moines, IA 50309

U.S. Marshal's Office
Property/Civil/Evidence Section
208 U.S. Courthouse
East 1st and Walnut
Des Moines, IA 50309
Please do not call for information. All sales are posted in advance at
the county courthouse.

U.S. Bankruptcy Court
318 U.S. Courthouse
Des Moines, IA 50309
Trustee handles sale. Please do not call.

WICHITA, KANSAS

HUD/FHA
110 North Market
Wichita, KS 67202

Veterans Administration
901 George Washington Blvd.
Wichita, KS 67211

U.S. Marshal's Office
Property/Civil/Evidence Section
401 North Market
Wichita, KS 67202
Check local paper for sale notices.

U.S. Bankruptcy Court
401 N. Market, Rm. 303
U.S. Courthouse
Wichita, KS 67202
Trustee handles sales.

LOUISVILLE, KENTUCKY

HUD/FHA
P.O. Box 1044
Louisville, KY 40201-1044

Farmers Home Administration
105 East Adams
LaGrange, KY 40031

Veterans Administration
600 Federal Road
Louisville, KY 40214

U.S. Marshal's Office
Property/Civil/Evidence Section
114 U.S. Courthouse
601 West Broadway
Louisville, KY 40202

U.S. Bankruptcy Court
414 U.S. Courthouse
601 W. Broadway
Louisville, KY 40202

NEW ORLEANS, LOUISIANA

HUD/FHA
1661 Canal St.
New Orleans, LA 70112

Farmers Home Administration
P.O. Box 7
Gretna, LA 70054

Veterans Administration
Regional Office
701 Loyola Avenue
New Orleans, LA 70113

U.S. Marshal's Office
Property/Civil/Evidence Section
U.S. Marshal's Office, Rm. 600
500 Camp
New Orleans, LA 70130
This agency has no mailing list. Check the *Times Picayune* for sale
  notices.

U.S. Bankruptcy Court
Eastern Louisiana Dist.
500 Camp St., Rm. 104
New Orleans, LA 70130-3386

AUGUSTA, MAINE

HUD/FHA
P.O. Box 1357
Bangor, ME 04401

Veterans Administration
V.A.M.R.O.C.
Togus, ME 04330

U.S. Marshal's Office
Property/Civil/Evidence Section
P.O. Box 349
Portland, ME 04112

U.S. Bankruptcy Court
P.O. Box 48-DTS
Portland, ME 04112

BALTIMORE, MARYLAND

HUD/FHA
Equitable Bldg.
10 N. Calvert St.
Baltimore, MD 21201

Farmers Home Administration
1004 Littlestown Pike
Westminster, MD 21157

Veterans Administration
G. H. Fallon Federal Bldg.
31 Hopkins Plaza
Baltimore, MD 21201

U.S. Marshal's Office
Property/Civil/Evidence Section
101 W. Lombard St., Rm. 605
Baltimore, MD 21201

U.S. Bankruptcy Court
Room 919
101 W. Lombard St.
Baltimore, MD 21201

BOSTON, MASSACHUSETTS

HUD/FHA
J.F.K. Federal Bldg.
Boston, MA 02203

Veterans Administration
J.F.K. Federal Bldg.
Boston, MA 02203

U.S. Marshal's Office
1516 Post Office Bldg.
Boston, MA 02203

U.S. Bankruptcy Court
10 Causeway St.
Boston, MA 02222-1093

DETROIT, MICHIGAN

HUD/FHA
McNamara Bldg.
477 Michigan Ave.
Detroit, MI 48226

Veterans Administration
McNamara Bldg.
477 Michigan Avenue
Detroit, MI 48226

204

U.S. Marshal's Office
Property/Civil/Evidence Section
120 Federal Bldg.
231 Lafayette Blvd.
Detroit, MI 48226
Check the *Detroit Legal News*.

U.S. Bankruptcy Court
1002 Federal Bldg.
231 West Lafayette Blvd.
Detroit, MI 48226

MINNEAPOLIS-ST. PAUL, MINNESOTA

HUD/FHA
200 South 2nd St.
Minneapolis, MN 55401

Farmers Home Administration
316 North Robert
St. Paul, MN 55101

Veterans Administration
Fort Snelling Federal Bldg.
St. Paul, MN 55111

U.S. Marshal's Office
Property/Civil/Evidence Section
110 South 4th St.
Minneapolis, MN 55401
Sales advertised in *Finance and Commerce*.

U.S. Bankruptcy Court
600 Galaxy Blvd.
330 2nd Ave. S.
Minneapolis, MN 55401

U.S. Bankruptcy Court
627 Federal Bldg.
316 N. Robert St.
St. Paul, MN 55101

JACKSON, MISSISSIPPI

HUD/FHA
Federal Bldg.
100 West Capitol Street
Jackson, MS 39269

Farmers Home Administration
Federal Bldg.
100 West Capitol Street
Jackson, MS 39269

Veterans Administration
Federal Bldg.
100 West Capitol Street
Jackson, MS 39269

U.S. Marshal's Office
Property/Civil/Evidence Section
U.S. Post Office & Courthouse
P.O. Box 959
Jackson, MS 39205
Sales are advertised in the *Clarion Ledger* and the *Jackson Daily News*.

U.S. Bankruptcy Court
P.O. Drawer 2448
Jackson, MS 39225-2448

KANSAS CITY, MISSOURI

HUD/FHA
1103 Grand
Kansas City, MO 64106

Veterans Administration
601 East 12th
Kansas City, MO 64106

U.S. Marshal's Office
Property/Civil/Evidence Section
811 Grand, Rm. 509
Kansas City, MO 64106
Check the *Kansas City Daily Record* for notices.

U.S. Bankruptcy Court
811 Grand, Rm. 913
Kansas City, MO 64106

ST. LOUIS, MISSOURI

HUD/FHA
210 North Tucker Blvd.
St. Louis, MO 63101

Farmers Home Administration
1520 Market
St. Louis, MO 63103

Veterans Administration
1520 Market
St. Louis, MO 63103

U.S. Marshal's Office
Property/Civil/Evidence Section
1114 Market St., Rm. 108
St. Louis, MO 63101
Check the *St. Louis Post Dispatch,* Saturday and Sunday, in the
classifieds under "Legal Section."

U.S. Bankruptcy Court
1114 Market St., Rm. 730
St. Louis, MO 63101

HELENA, MONTANA

HUD/FHA
Drawer 10095, Federal Bldg.
Helena, MT 59626

Veterans Administration
VA Center
Fort Harrison, MT 59636

U.S. Marshal's Office
Property/Civil/Evidence Section
P.O. Box 2179
Billings, MT 59103
Check local paper in county where property is located. Also posted at
the courthouse.

U.S. Bankruptcy Court
Great Falls Post Office Bldg., Rm. 25
Great Falls, MT 59401

OMAHA, NEBRASKA

HUD/FHA
7100 W. Center Rd.
Omaha, NE 68106

Farmers Home Administration
4734 S. 131st
Omaha, NE 68137

Veterans Administration
100 Centennial Mall N.
Lincoln, NE 68501

U.S. Marshal's Office
Property/Civil/Evidence Section
215 N. 17th
Omaha, NE 68102

U.S. Bankruptcy Court
Box 428 Downtown Station
Omaha, NE 68101

LAS VEGAS, NEVADA

HUD/FHA
720 S. 7th
Las Vegas, NV 89101

Farmers Home Administration
300 S. Las Vegas Blvd.
Las Vegas, NV 89101

Veterans Administration
245 Liberty
Reno, NV 89520

U.S. Bankruptcy Court
300 Las Vegas Blvd.
P.O. Box 16018
Las Vegas, NV 89101

CONCORD, NEW HAMPSHIRE

HUD/FHA
275 Chestnut St.
Manchester, NH 03131-2487

Veterans Administration
275 Chestnut
Norris Cotton Federal Bldg.
Manchester, NH 03101

U.S. Marshal's Office
Property/Civil/Evidence Section
P.O. Box 1435
Concord, NH 03301

U.S. Bankruptcy Court
Merrimack County Courthouse
163 N. Main St.
P.O. Box 1417
Concord, NH 03301

NEWARK, NEW JERSEY

HUD/FHA
60 Park Pl.
Newark, NJ 07109

Veterans Administration
20 Washington Pl.
Newark, NJ 07102

U.S. Marshal's Office
Property/Civil/Evidence Section
Civil Section
P.O. Box 186
Newark, NJ 07107

U.S. Bankruptcy Court
P.O. Box 557
Newark, NJ 07101

ALBUQUERQUE, NEW MEXICO

HUD/FHA
825 Truman N.E.
Albuquerque, NM 87110

Farmers Home Administration
3520 Pan American Fwy. N.E.
Albuquerque, NM 87101

Veterans Administration
500 Gold Ave. S.W.
Albuquerque, NM 87102

U.S. Marshal's Office
Property/Civil/Evidence Section
301 Grand N.E.
Albuquerque, NM 87102

U.S. Bankruptcy Court
P.O. Box 546
Albuquerque, NM 87103

NEW YORK, NEW YORK

HUD/FHA
26 Federal Plaza
New York, NY 10278

Veterans Administration
252 7th Ave.
New York, NY 10001

U.S. Marshal's Office
Property/Civil/Evidence Section
1 Saint Andrew's Plaza
New York, NY 10007

U.S. Bankruptcy Court
2nd Fl., Rm. 230
U.S. Courthouse
40 Bowie Square
New York, NY 10007

ROCHESTER, NEW YORK

HUD/FHA
316 Federal Blvd.
Rochester, NY 14609

Veterans Administration
100 State St.
Rochester, NY 14614

U.S. Marshal's Office
Property/Civil/Evidence Section
100 State St.
Rochester, NY 14614

U.S. Bankruptcy Court
212 U.S. Courthouse
100 State St.
Rochester, NY 14614

GREENSBORO, NORTH CAROLINA

HUD/FHA
415 North Edgeworth Street
Greensboro, NC 27401

Farmers Home Administration
324 Market St.
Greensboro, NC 27401

Veterans Administration
501 Rock Quarry Rd.
Raleigh, NC 27401

U.S. Marshal's Office
Property/Civil/Evidence Section
324 West Market St.
Greensboro, NC 27401

U.S. Bankruptcy Court
P.O. Box 26100
Greensboro, NC 27402-6100

BISMARCK, NORTH DAKOTA

HUD/FHA
P.O. Box 2483
Fargo, ND 58108

Veterans Administration
Ft. Snelling Federal Bldg.
St. Paul, MN 55111

U.S. Marshal's Office
Property/Civil/Evidence Section
P.O. Box 5007
Bismarck, ND 58502

U.S. Bankruptcy Court
P.O. Box 1110
Fargo, ND 58107
Check local papers for sale notices.

CINCINNATI, OHIO

HUD/FHA
Federal Office Bldg., Rm. 9002
550 Main St.
Cincinnati, OH 45202

Veterans Administration
Federal Office Bldg.
550 Main St.
Cincinnati, OH 45202

U.S. Marshal's Office
Property/Civil/Evidence Section
P.O. Box 688
Cincinnati, OH 45201

U.S. Bankruptcy Court
735 U.S. Post Office and Courthouse
Cincinnati, OH 45202-3981

CLEVELAND, OHIO

HUD/FHA
1375 Euclid
Cleveland, OH 44115

Veterans Administration
1240 E. 9th
Cleveland, OH 44114

U.S. Marshal's Office
Property/Civil/Evidence Section
201 Superior Ave.
Cleveland, OH 44114

U.S. Bankruptcy Court
Superior of Public Square
Cleveland, OH 44114
Check local newspapers for sale notices.

OKLAHOMA CITY, OKLAHOMA

HUD/FHA
200 N.W. Fifth
Oklahoma City, OK 73102

Farmers Home Administration
3945 S.E. 15th
Oklahoma City, OK 73115

Veterans Administration
125 S. Main
Muskogee, OK 74401

U.S. Marshal's Office
Property/Civil/Evidence Section
200 N.W. 4th
Oklahoma City, OK 73102

U.S. Bankruptcy Court
201 Dean A. McGee Ave.
Oklahoma City, OK 73102

PORTLAND, OREGON

HUD/FHA
520 S.W. 6th
Portland, OR 97204

Farmers Home Administration
1220 S.W. 3rd
Portland, OR 97204

Veterans Administration
1220 S.W. 3rd
Portland, OR 97204

U.S. Marshal's Office
Property/Civil/Evidence Section
U.S. Courthouse
620 S.W. Main St.
Portland, OR 97204

U.S. Bankruptcy Court
900 Orbanco Bldg.
1001 S.W. 5th Ave.
Portland, OR 97204
Check local newspapers for sale notices.

PHILADELPHIA, PENNSYLVANIA

HUD/FHA
105 S. 7th St.
Philadelphia, PA 19106

Farmers Home Administration
R.D. 3, Route 19
Waterford, PA 16441

Veterans Administration
5601 Broad St., Rm. 202
Philadelphia, PA 19141

U.S. Marshal's Office
Property/Civil/Evidence Section
601 Market, Rm. 2110
Philadelphia, PA 19106
Check local newspapers for sale notices.

U.S. Bankruptcy Court
601 Market St., Rm. 3726
Philadelphia, PA 19106

PITTSBURGH, PENNSYLVANIA

HUD/FHA
7th & Grant St.
Pittsburgh, PA 15219

Farmers Home Administration
37 Highland Ave.
Washington, PA

Veterans Administration
1000 Liberty Ave.
Pittsburgh, PA 15222

U.S. Marshal's Office
Property/Civil/Evidence Section
539 U.S. Courthouse
Pittsburgh, PA 15219
Check local paper for sale notices.

U.S. Bankruptcy Court
1602 Federal Bldg.
1000 Liberty Ave.
Pittsburgh, PA 15222

PROVIDENCE, RHODE ISLAND

HUD/FHA
330 John O. Pastore Federal Bldg.
Providence, RI 02903

Farmers Home Administration
48 Quakerlane
West Warwick, RI 02893

Veterans Administration
321 S. Main
Providence, RI 02917

U.S. Marshal's Office
Property/Civil/Evidence Section
303 Federal Bldg.
U.S. Courthouse
Providence, RI 02901
Sale notices are in the *Providence Journal* in the "Legal Notices" section.

U.S. Bankruptcy Court
Federal Center
380 Westminster Mall
Providence, RI 02903

COLUMBIA, SOUTH CAROLINA

HUD/FHA
Strom Thurmond Federal Bldg.
1835 Assembly St.
Columbia, SC 29201

Farmers Home Administration
1835 Assembly St.
Columbia, SC 29201

Veterans Administration
1801 Assembly St.
Columbia, SC 29201

U.S. Marshal's Office
Property/Civil/Evidence Section
Civil Division
P.O. Box 1774
Columbia, SC 29202

U.S. Bankruptcy Court
P.O. Box 1448
Columbia, SC 29202
Please do not call for information. They charge for response by mail.
   The best way to find out about periodic sales is to check your local
   paper for notices.

PIERRE, SOUTH DAKOTA

HUD/FHA
The Denver regional office handles FHA business for South Dakota.
   Foreclosed houses are listed in local newspapers on Saturday and
   Sunday. See property with Realtor of your choice and have him fill
   out bid on properties of interest. Then submit bid to HUD.

Veterans Administration
Contact regional office in St. Paul:
Bishop Henry Whipple Federal Bldg.
Ft. Snelling
St. Paul, MN 55111

U.S. Marshal's Office
Property/Civil/Evidence Section
P.O. Box 397
Pierre, SD 57501

U.S. Bankruptcy Court
P.O. Box 5060
Sioux Falls, SD 57117
Check local newspapers for sale notices.

NASHVILLE, TENNESSEE

HUD/FHA
1 Commercial St., Su. 1600
Nashville, TN 37239-1600

Veterans Administration
110 Ninth Ave. S.
Nashville, TN 37203

U.S. Marshal's Office
Property/Civil/Evidence Section
866 U.S. Courthouse
Nashville, TN 37201

U.S. Bankruptcy Court
701 Broadway
207 Customs House
Nashville, TN 37203

HOUSTON, TEXAS

HUD/FHA
2211 Norfolk, Su. 200
Houston, TX 77098-4096

217

Veterans Administration
2215 Murworth
Houston, TX 77054

U.S. Marshal's Office
Property/Civil/Evidence Section
P.O. Box 61608
Houston, TX 77208
Sales advertised in the *Houston Order Post* and the *Houston Chronicle*.

U.S. Bankruptcy Court
515 Rusk
Houston, TX 77002

SALT LAKE CITY, UTAH

HUD/FHA
324 South State St., Su. 220
Salt Lake City, UT 84111

Veterans Administration
125 S. State St.
P.O. Box 11500
Salt Lake City, UT 84111

U.S. Marshal's Office
Property/Civil/Evidence Section
P.O. Box 1234
Salt Lake City, UT 84110

U.S. Bankruptcy Court
350 S. Main St., Rm. 361
Salt Lake City, UT 84101

MONTPELIER, VERMONT

HUD/FHA
275 Chestnut
Manchester, NH 03103

Veterans Administration
North Hartland Rd.
White River Junction, VT 05001

U.S. Marshal's Office
Property/Civil/Evidence Section
Montpelier, VT 05602

U.S. Bankruptcy Court
P.O. Box 6648
Rutland, VT 05701

RICHMOND, VIRGINIA

HUD/FHA
701 East Franklin St., Rm. 412
Richmond, VA 23219

Veterans Administration
210 Franklin Road S.W.
Roanoke, VA 24011

U.S. Marshal's Office
Property/Civil/Evidence Section
P.O. Box 2G
Richmond, VA 23203
Sales are handled out of the Alexandria office. Check *The Washington Post* or the *Richmond Times Leader* or other local papers.

U.S. Bankruptcy Court
P.O. Box 676
Richmond, VA 23206

SEATTLE, WASHINGTON

HUD/FHA
Arcade Plaza
1321 Second Ave.
Seattle, WA 98101-2054

Veterans Administration
915 Second Ave.
Seattle, WA 98174

U.S. Marshal's Office
Property/Civil/Evidence Section
P.O. Box 302
Jackson Federal Bldg.
915 Second Ave.
Seattle, WA 98714

U.S. Bankruptcy Court
1010 Fifth Ave.
Seattle, WA 98104

CHARLESTON, WEST VIRGINIA

HUD/FHA
Kanawha Valley Bldg., Lower Level
405 Capitol St., Su. 708
Charleston, WV 25301-1795

Veterans Administration
605 Atlas Bldg.
Charleston, WV 25301

U.S. Marshal's Office
Property/Civil/Evidence Section
P.O. Box 267
Charleston, WV 25330

U.S. Bankruptcy Court
500 Quarrier St.
Charleston, WV 25301
Clerks have no information on sales. Check local papers.

MADISON, WISCONSIN

HUD/FHA
310 W. Wisconsin Ave., Su. 1380
Milwaukee, WI 53203-2289

Veterans Administration
3400 Wisconsin Ave.
Milwaukee, WI 53208

U.S. Marshal's Office
Marshal's Office holds no sales.

U.S. Bankruptcy Court
P.O. Box 548
Madison, WI 53701

CHEYENNE, WYOMING

HUD/FHA
P.O. Box 580
Casper, WY 82602

Veterans Administration
44 Union Blvd.
Box 25126
Denver, CO 80225

U.S. Marshal's Office
Property/Civil/Evidence Section
P.O. Box 768
Cheyenne, WY 82003

U.S. Bankruptcy Court
P.O. Box 1107
Cheyenne, WY 82003

Cash Flow Tools

Lease-option, equity-sharing, and combined lease-option/equity-sharing agreements are excellent tools that allow investors to control property without tying up large amounts of cash. They enable you to invest in profitable real estate and generate positive cash flows using very little capital. Since many people who are interested in these agreements have never seen how the contracts for them are written, I've included samples of each here.

I must point out, however, that these samples are for illustration only. Some clauses or provisions may not be enforceable in particular states or cities or may not be suitable for the deal you have in mind. Therefore, before you attempt to use them, have them reviewed and adapted to your purposes by an attorney or other competent real estate professional who is familiar with your local laws and regulations.

RESIDENTIAL LEASE WITH OPTION TO PURCHASE

THIS AGREEMENT is made _____
between _____ and _____
(husband and wife), hereinafter called LESSEE/BUYER, and _____
and _____ (husband and wife/ _____), hereinafter called
LESSOR/SELLER.

1. SUBJECT PROPERTY:

(a) Lessor/Seller hereby leases to Lessee/Buyer that certain real property known as _____ and which is more particularly described as:

2. TERM:

(a) The term of this lease shall be for a period of- _____ year(s), commencing on the _____ day of _____ , 198 _____ , and ending on the _____ day of _____ , 19 _____ .

3. RENT:

(a) Lessee/Buyer shall pay Lessor/Seller as rent for subject premises the sum of $ _____ per month, commencing on the _____ day of _____ , 198 _____ , and a like amount to be due on the _____ day of each succeeding month during the term hereof. Payment shall be presented to Lessor/Seller or their agent or assignee at _____ or a designated place.

4. POSSESSION:

(a) Possession will be/was delivered to Lessee/Buyer on _____

5. OPTION TO PURCHASE:

(a) Lessor/Seller grants to Lessee/Buyer, subject to the provisions of Paragraphs 7 and 8 the right to purchase at any time during the time period of _____ , 19 _____ through _____ , 19 _____ said property conditioned upon full compliance by Lessee/Buyer with all terms of this Agreement.

(b) Lessee/Buyer agrees to pay $ _____ to Lessor/Seller in lawful U.S. currency as consideration for Lessor/Seller granting Lessee/Buyer an option to purchase said property. This consideration shall be paid as follows: $ _____ prior to occupancy, or _____ (this amount is in addition to the rent as specified in Paragraph 3 above). Lessor/Seller agrees that upon exercise of the option Lessee/Buyer shall be credited with $ _____ from each monthly rental payment of $ _____ (as specified in Paragraph 3 above) toward the option consideration. SHOULD THE OPTION NOT BE EXERCISED BY LESSEE/BUYER, THERE WILL BE NO REFUND OF ANY OPTION CONSIDERATION.

224

(c) The purchase price of the property shall be in an amount agreed upon by Lessor/Seller and Lessee/Buyer. In the event Lessor/Seller and Lessee/Buyer are unable to agree upon a purchase price, then the fair market value (purchase price) of the property shall be determined under provisions of Paragraph 25. In no event shall the purchase price be less than the initial agreed upon value of the property or $ _____ .

(d) At such time as the option is exercised, Lessor/Seller will credit Lessee/Buyer with one-half of any increase in value of the property that accrues between the date of this agreement and the date that the Lessee/Buyer notifies Lessor/Seller of their intent to exercise the option. The increase in value shall be measured as the difference between the value of the property as of _____ , i.e., $ _____ and the purchase price when the option is exercised.

6. ENCUMBRANCES:

(a) The only encumbrance(s) against said property is(are):

The parties agree that neither will cause or permit any lien to attach to or exist on or against the subject property which shall or may be superior to the rights of either party or to encumber the property in any manner without having obtained the written consent of the other.

(b) Prior to the exercise of the option, Lessor/Seller reserves the right to change existing encumbrances on the property through refinance, early payoff of the loan(s), or modifications of existing loans so long as said change would not create an encumbrance exceeding the agreed upon value of the property as of _____ (date), i.e., $ _____ . In the event of a refinance or modification, Lessee/Buyer agrees to subordinate their equitable interest so long as the modification or new encumbrance is fully amortized over at least 15 years and does not exceed _____ fixed rate interest or _____ initial variable rate of interest.

7. EXERCISE OF OPTION:

(a) The option may be exercised by Lessee/Buyer, if at all, as long as Lessee/Buyer is not in default of the terms and conditions of this agreement as enumerated under Paragraph 18. To exercise the option, Lessee/Buyer must notify Lessor/Seller in writing of such acceptance. Lessee/Buyer should mail the notification to Lessor/Seller at _____ or a designated place. The postmark must be no later than _____.

8. TITLE:

(a) Within five (5) days upon receipt of written notification by Lessee/Buyer to exercise the option, Lessor/Seller shall execute and deliver to _____ all documents required to transfer title to subject real property along with appropriate escrow instruction. Escrow shall be deemed "open" as of the date of Lessor/Seller's delivery.

(b) Lessee/Buyer's duty to perform hereunder, after exercise of the option, is contingent upon title to the property being insurable as free and clear of all liens, encumbrances or other clouds on title to the property, except:

(1) General and special taxes for the fiscal year in which the escrow closes:

(2) Exceptions, as agreed by Lessee/Buyer, to be contained in the title report and all current easements, covenants and restrictions of record.

(c) Lessee/Buyer shall have fifteen (15) days from receipt of a title report to examine the title to the property and to report in writing any valid objections thereto. Any exceptions to the title which would be disclosed by examination of the record shall be deemed to have been accepted unless reported in writing within said fifteen (15) days. If Lessee/Buyer objects to any exceptions to the title, Lessor/Seller shall use due diligence to remove such exceptions at their expense before close of escrow. But if such exceptions cannot be removed before close of escrow, all rights and obligations hereunder may, at the election of the Lessee/Buyer, terminate and end. Should Lessee/Buyer elect to rescind the contract because of title exceptions, Lessor/Seller shall refund the option consideration as follows: $ _____ plus any amounts paid by Lessee/Buyer in excess of the fair and reasonable monthly rental as specified in Paragraph 20, "Holding Over." At the expiration of said fifteen (15) day period for examination of title, Lessee/Buyer shall be deemed to have accepted such title in the absence of the required written objections.

9. ESCROW:

(a) Upon both parties' agreement to consummate the sale, appropriate documents shall be recorded and escrow shall close within 45 days from the opening thereof. If escrow is not closed prior to the scheduled closing date or Lessee/Buyer has not complied with the terms of this agreement within forty-five (45) days after escrow is opened, escrow shall be cancelled and this agreement shall be null and void. Lessee/Buyer, Lessor/Seller or escrow holder, as applicable, shall perform the following duties prior to close of escrow:

(1) Lessor/Seller shall deliver to escrow holder an executed grant deed to the property in recordable form conveying title in the property to Lessee/Buyer.

(2) Escrow holder shall credit Lessee/Buyer with the OPTION CONSIDERATION accumulated and held by Lessor/Seller during the option period and said option consideration so credited and appreciation (as per Paragraph 5 (d)), shall be deducted from purchase price.

(b) In the event Lessee/Buyer shall have exercised the option in the manner aforementioned herein, and Lessee/Buyer shall not have closed this escrow on the Scheduled Closing Date for a reason other than Lessor/Seller's failure to deliver a grant deed to escrow holder as required by Paragraph 9 (a) (1) above, or the inability of escrow holder to obtain a policy of title insurance to insure title in Lessee/Buyer, subject only to those exceptions to title described in the policy of title or as otherwise described in Paragraph 8 (a) above, then: (1) Lessee/Buyer shall have no right, title or interest in the property; (2) Lessee/Buyer shall be liable to Lessor/Seller for all damages caused by Lessor/Seller's wrongful failure to close escrow unless Lessor/Seller shall be in breach; (3) This escrow shall be automatically terminated without further instructions from any party hereto; and (4) Escrow holder shall return all items to the party who deposited such items into escrow, without further instructions from either party hereto. Notwithstanding the above, Lessor/Seller may demand that Lessee/Buyer execute cancellation instructions prepared by escrow holder in the event an escrow established pursuant hereto is not closed on or before the Scheduled Closing Date, for a reason other than described in this paragraph.

10. PROBATIONS, CLOSING COSTS, ASSUMPTION AND REFINANCING COSTS:

(a) Real property taxes on the property and general and special assessments, if any, for the current fiscal year shall be prorated to the close of escrow.

(b) The ''closing costs'' shall be those costs incurred in conjunction with closing escrow and shall be paid at the close of escrow as follows:

227

(1) All closing costs shall be paid one-half by Lessor/Seller and one-half by Lessee/Buyer except all assumption fees imposed by the secured lien holder(s) set forth in Paragraph 5, if Lessee/Buyer elects to formally assume said loan(s) of record, shall be paid fully by Lessee/Buyer.

(2) Any charges, prepayment penalties or expenses imposed by the terms of the underlying Deed of Trust(s) and promissory note(s) of the lien holder set forth in Paragraph 5 in the event Lessee/Buyer elects to refinance or to pay off said encumbrance shall be paid by Lessee/Buyer.

(3) In the event escrow does not close on the Scheduled Closing Date or another mutually agreed upon date thereafter, the closing costs incurred through the escrow to such date shall be the responsibility of the party at fault. In the event escrow shall fail to close on the Scheduled Closing Date or another mutually agreed upon closing date due to fault of **both** parties or **neither** party to this agreement, the costs of terminating the escrow shall be divided equally between the parties.

11. ACCELERATION OF PAYMENT:

12. REPAIRS AND CONDITION OF PROPERTY DURING LEASE PERIOD:

(a) Lessee/Buyer accepts the premises as being in good condition and repair. Lessee/Buyer, at Lessee/Buyer's cost and without obligation to Lessor/Seller shall keep and maintain the premises, and every part thereof, in good and satisfactory repair and condition, reasonable wear and tear excepted, during the term of the lease. Buyer shall make no major changes, improvements or repairs to the property without first obtaining the written approval of Lessor/Seller. Lessee/Buyer shall indemnify and hold Lessor/Seller harmless from any and all mechanics liens or claims of lien and all attorneys fees, costs and expenses which may accrue, grow out of, or be incurred by reason of or on account of such lien or claim of lien.

(b) Subject property is represented by Lessor/Seller to Lessee/Buyer as having no physical defects of which Lessor/Seller is aware, that are of a magnitude that should be disclosed to Lessee/Buyer except:

13. INDEMNIFICATION:

(a) Lessor/Seller shall not be liable for any damage or injury to Lessee/Buyer or any other person, or to any property, occurring on the premises, or any part thereof, or in common areas thereof, unless such damage is the approximate result of the negligence or unlawful act of

228

Lessor/Seller, their agents or employees. Lessee/Buyer agrees to hold Lessor/Seller harmless from any claims for damages no matter how caused, except for injury or damages for which Lessor/Seller is legally responsible, so long as Lessee/Buyer remains in possession of the premises.

14. UTILITIES:

(a) Lessor/Seller shall maintain a policy of fire insurance in the amount of $ _____ insuring the premises from loss by fire, flood, earthquake or other disaster during the lease period and to close of escrow. Any loss to the real property or personal property (exclusive of Lessee/Buyer's furnishings and personal belongings) contained therein for any reason whatsoever, including condemnation by any governmental agency, fire, flood, earthquake, or whatever, which is not covered by Lessor/Seller's policy of insurance, will be apportioned between the parties as to their interests pursuant to this agreement.

16. ORDINANCES AND STATUTES:

(a) Lessee/Buyer shall comply with all statutes, ordinances and requirements of all municipal, state and federal authorities now in force, or which may hereafter be in force, pertaining to the use of the premises.

17. LATE CHARGES:

(a) Lessee/Buyer acknowledges that late payment of rent will cause Lessor/Seller to incur costs not contemplated by this lease, the exact amount of which is extremely difficult to ascertain. If any installment of rent is more than TEN (10) days past due, Lessee/Buyer shall pay Lessor/Seller a late charge equal to 5% of such past due amount. The parties agree that such late charge represents a fair and reasonable estimate of the costs Lessor/Seller incurred for extra accounting charges imposed by lenders of record.

18. DEFAULT:

(a) The occurrence of any of the following shall constitute a material default and breach of lease by Lessee/Buyer.

(1) Monthly lease payments must be paid in a timely fashion, i.e., on or before the 1st day of each month. If Lessee/Buyer is more than TEN (10) days late on more than three of the monthly payments and Lessor/Seller has not agreed in writing to extensions on the appropriate due dates, Lessor/Seller will treat the failure to pay in a timely fashion as a

breach of condition of the contract and may refuse to convey title, even if there are no payments in default at the time Lessee/Buyer attempts to exercise the option to purchase. If the lease is in substantial default (90% or more of any monthly increment past due) at the time the option period matures, Lessor/Seller may refuse to convey title. CREDITWORTHI-NESS OF LESSEE/BUYER IS OF THE ESSENCE IN THE LEASE-OPTION PORTION OF THIS CONTRACT. CREDITWORTHINESS WILL BE BASED UPON LESSEE/BUYER'S REGULAR AND TIMELY PAYMENTS OF MONTHLY LEASE OBLIGATIONS AS SPECIFIED ABOVE.

(2) Any failure by Lessee/Buyer to perform any other provision of this lease to be performed by Lessee/Buyer where such failure continues THIRTY (30) days after written notice thereof by Lessor/Seller will constitute a material breach of this contract.

19. REMEDIES UPON DEFAULT:

(a) In the event of any such default by Lessee/Buyer, then in addition to any other remedies available to Lessor/Seller at law or in equity, Lessor/Seller shall have the option to terminate this lease and all rights hereunder by giving written notice of intention to terminate.

20. HOLDING OVER:

(a) Any holding over after the expiration of the term of the lease in the event Lessee/Buyer's option to purchase is not exercised or upon the exercise of Lessor/Seller's option to terminate the lease pursuant to the Default provisions of Paragraphs 15 and 16, shall be construed to be a tenancy from month to month at a monthly rental of $ _____ . The parties have bargained for and agree that said monthly sum of $ _____ is a fair and reasonable monthly rental for the subject premises and a sum which would have been reasonably used as a lease/rental amount during the term thereof except for the negotiated anticipation of the parties that Lessee/Buyer would exercise the option to purchase prior to termination.

21. NOTICES:

(a) Any and all notices and other communications required or permitted by this agreement shall be served on or given to either party by the other party in writing and shall be deemed duly served and given when personally delivered to any of the parties to whom it is directed, or in lieu of such personal service, when deposited in the United

States mail first class postage prepaid, addressed to Lessor/Seller at
_____ or Lessee/Buyer at the property address or such forwarding address that Lessee/Buyer has given to Lessor/Seller.

22. ASSIGNMENT:

(a) Lessee/Buyer shall not assign, sublet, transfer, mortgage, pledge, hypothecate or encumber this lease, or any interest in it without written permission of Lessor/Seller. Written permission prior to assigning, subletting, transferring, mortgaging, pledging, hypothecating or encumbering this lease is a condition precedent to the validity of same.

23. WAIVER:

(a) The waiver by Lessor/Seller of any provision of this agreement shall not constitute a waiver of any other provision of this agreement or any future waiver of the same provision.

24. ARBITRATION:

(a) Any controversy between the parties to this Agreement involving the construction or application of any of the terms, provisions, or conditions of this Agreement, shall on the written request of either party served on the other be submitted to arbitration and such arbitration shall comply with and be governed by the provisions of the California Arbitration Act, Sections 1280–1294.2 of the California Code of Civil Procedure. The parties shall each appoint one person to hear and determine the dispute, and if they are unable to agree, then the two persons so chosen shall select a third impartial arbitrator whose decision shall be final and conclusive upon both parties. The cost of arbitration shall be borne by the losing party or in such proportions as the arbitrator shall decide.

25. APPRAISAL:

(a) When necessary, the fair market value shall be determined as the average of two appraisals of the property as described in this paragraph. If possible, the appraisals shall be based on the sale prices of comparable properties in the market area sold within the preceding three-month period. The appraisals shall be made upon request of either party by two independent residential appraisers, one to be selected by Lessor/Seller and one by Lessee/Buyer. Each appraiser shall be approved by the Federal National Mortgage Association. The cost of the appraiser selected by Lessor/Seller shall be borne by Lessor/Seller, and the cost of the appraiser selected by

231

Lessee/Buyer shall be borne by Lessee/Buyer. The fair market value of the property shall be determined as the average of the two appraisals. If Lessee/Buyer fails to select a qualified appraiser within 15 days after Lessor/Seller has notified Lessee/Buyer in writing of Lessor/Seller's request for an appraisal of the property, the reasons therefore, and Lessee/Buyer's option to select an independent appraiser within 15 days after Lessor/Seller's request is submitted to Lessee/Buyer, Lessor/Seller may designate the second appraiser, provided Lessor/Seller's request informs Lessee/Buyer of this time limitation, and that Lessor/Seller will select an appraiser on behalf of Lessee/Buyer in the event Lessee/Buyer fails to designate an appraiser, with consequent cost to Lessee/Buyer. If pursuant to this section Lessor/Seller designates the second appraiser, the cost of both appraisals shall be borne equally by Lessor/Seller and Lessee/Buyer. If in any case the property has been damaged (other than normal wear and tear) and the damage has not been fully repaired, the determination of fair market value shall be based on the condition of the property not including the damage. Nothing in this paragraph shall preclude Lessor/Seller and Lessee/Buyer from establishing fair market value of the property by mutual agreement in lieu of appraisals pursuant to this section.

26. ATTORNEYS' FEES:

(a) In the event any legal action is brought by either party to enforce the terms hereof or relating to the demised premises, the prevailing party shall be entitled to all costs incurred in connection with such action, including reasonable attorneys' fees as determined by the Court.

27. BROKER'S AGENCY:

(a) A licensed California Real Estate Broker, the agent guiding this transaction, is employed solely by Lessor/Seller as a single agent Consultant on an hourly fee basis and, as such, represents their interest only, other than certain divided interests within ethical parameters, which are required by law.

28. TIME:

(a) Time is of the essence in this lease and the options given hereunder.

29. GENDER, TENSE AND PLURALITY OF WORDS:

(a) All words used in this Agreement, including the words Lessor/Seller and Lessee/Buyer shall be construed to include the plural as well as the singular number; words used herein in the present tense shall include the future as well as the present, and words used in the masculine gender shall include the feminine and neuter.

30. MODIFICATION:

(a) Any modification of any portion of this Agreement must be made in writing and signed by both parties.

31. RECORDING:

(a) If Lessee/Buyer chooses to record a memorandum of this Agreement or the Agreement in its entirety, Lessor/Seller shall bear such costs. Lessee/Buyer shall also, prior to said recording, sign a Quit Claim Deed and escrow instructions to (Title Company) to be held by said title company as a neutral third party which will provide means to clear title to the property should Lessee/Buyer terminate this agreement for any reason prior to exercise of the option.

DATED: _____   _____

_____

_____

_____

EQUITY-SHARING CONTRACT

THIS AGREEMENT entered into this _____ day of _____ , 19 _____ , by and between _____ , hereinafter referred to as Investor and _____ , hereinafter referred to as Co-Investor.

WHEREAS, _____ now owns the property located at _____ and described as:

_____
_____
_____
_____
_____
_____
_____

and wishes to sell an undivided one-half interest in such property to
_____ as tenants in common, and

WHEREAS, the parties desire to provide for the financing, management and disposition of such property.

IT IS, THEREFORE, agreed as follows:

1. **TERM OF AGREEMENT**

The term of the Agreement shall be for a period of _____ months unless otherwise agreed upon.

2. **VALUE OF PROPERTY**

The value of said property was appraised and agreed to be One Hundred Thirty Thousand and no/100 Dollars ($130,000).

3. **INVESTOR'S INVESTMENT**

The Investor's investment, including closing costs, on such property shall have been taken in his name, subject to required documents and security documents. Investor shall convey to Co-Investor an undivided one-half interest in such property, conditioned upon full compliance by Co-Investor with all of the terms of this Agreement. Investor's investment is approximately Thirty Thousand and no/100 Dollars ($30,000).*
*Depends on actual balances of Notes and Deeds of Trust now existing on said property.

4. **CONSIDERATION FOR AND CONDITIONS OF CO-INVESTOR'S PURCHASE OF ONE-HALF INTEREST**

(a) Co-Investor acknowledges that his one-half interest in the property is subject to Notes and Deeds of Trust securing said property in the approximate amount of One Hundred Thousand Dollars ($100,000).

(b) Co-Investor agrees to pay the Investor, for the term of this Agreement, monthly payments of One Thousand Dollars ($1,000) including three Notes and Deeds of Trust as follows:

(1) Note and First Trust Deed in the amount of approximately $68,000, payable monthly at $591.68 including interest at 10.25%, Suburban Coastal lender, 30-year term.

(2) Note and Second Trust Deed in the amount of approximately $26,000, payable monthly at $409.67 including 18.50% interest, Security Pacific lender, 20-year loan.

(3) Note and Third Trust Deed in the amount of approximately $6,000 payable monthly at $150, including 10% interest, private lender, no due date.

(a) Taxes on property are in two installments of $451.09 for a total tax bill of $902.04 per year.

(b) Insurance is with State Farm, Homeowner's Policy, full

234

coverage, payable once a year in the amount of approximately $402.00. Monthly payments shall be based on the actual amount of payments due on all notes encumbering property along with 1/12th of the annual taxes and insurance. Said payment may increase or decrease in amount, depending on the type of existing financing or any variance in taxes or insurance. Payments shall be due on the first day of every month and shall be delinquent if not received by the holder of notes or his designees by the fifth day of every month.

Said monthly payment shall be credited as follows: One half of the payment shall be deemed to be a purchase payment to Investor for Co-Investor's one-half interest in the property. The remaining one-half payment shall be a lease payment to the Investor for the one-half interest retained by him in the property. Any partial or late payments shall be applied first to the late charges under Paragraph 7, secondly to rent, and any remainder to monthly purchase payments. The Co-Investors shall make all monthly payments to all beneficiaries and for taxes and insurance upon receipt of the monthly, quarterly, semiannual, or annual request for payment.

(c) Co-Investor agrees to execute a Deed of Trust in favor of Investor for the purpose of securing

(1) Payment to Investor of the indebtedness set forth in Paragraph 4 above.

(2) The performance of each agreement of Co-Investor incorporated by reference or contained herein. Deed of Trust is to name Yosemite Title Company as Trustee.

(d) Co-Investor agrees to maintain said property at his sole expense and not make any structural improvements without the written consent of the Investors.

(e) Co-Investor shall not dispose of any real or personal property connected with the home without written consent of the Investor.

(f) Co-Investor agrees to sign a lease agreement for Investor's one-half interest for 36 months, or until the property is sold, unless terminated earlier with the consent of Investor or by the purchase by Co-Investor of Investor's interest in the property. Said lease is attached hereto as Exhibit A and is fully incorporated herein.

(g) At the signing of this Agreement, Co-Investor shall pay for a one-year Homeowners Insurance Policy naming Investor as a Co-Insured. Fire insurance coverage shall not be less than One Hundred Thirty Thousand Dollars ($130,000). In the event of a total loss, Co-Investor shall assign his interest of any monies paid by the insurance company to the

235

Investor to cover his investment, including closing costs, as set forth in Paragraph 3. Any excess monies will be divided equally between the Investor and Co-Investor. In the event of a loss of any personal property, Investor agrees to assign his interest of any monies paid by the insurance company to the Co-Investor.

5. ENCUMBRANCES AND ASSIGNMENTS

Co-Investor shall not sell, transfer, assign, or encumber his interest in the property, this Agreement, or his lease of the property without the prior written consent of the Investor.

6. DEFAULT BY CO-INVESTOR

The occurrence of any of the following shall constitute a default by Co-Investor:

(a) Failure to make any payment under Paragraph 4 (b) when due, if the failure continues for ten (10) days after notice has been given to the Co-Investor.

(b) Abandonment and vacation of the premises (failure to occupy the premises for ten [10] consecutive days shall be deemed abandonment and vacation, unless notice to Investor is given in advance).

(c) Failure to perform any other provision of this Agreement and Exhibit A if the failure to perform is not cured within ten (10) days after notice has been given by Investor.

Notices given under this paragraph shall specify the alleged default and the applicable Agreement provisions, and shall demand that the Co-Investor perform the provisions of this Agreement or make the lease or purchase payment that is in arrears, as the case may be, within the applicable period of time, or quit the premises. No such notice shall be deemed a forfeiture or a termination of this Agreement unless Investor so elects in the notice.

7. INVESTOR'S REMEDIES IN CASE OF DEFAULT

Investor shall have the following remedies if Co-Investor commits default. These remedies are not exclusive, they are cumulative in addition to any remedies now or later allowed by law.

(a) If Co-Investor commits any default under Paragraph 6 herein, Investor may terminate the lease provisions of this Agreement and regain possession of the premises in the manner provided by the laws of unlawful detainer in the state of California in effect at the date of such default. Co-Investor agrees that his right to possession of the premises shall terminate by such default, notwithstanding his ownership interest in one-half of the premises. At Investor's option, he may continue the lease provisions of this Agreement in effect for so long as Investor does not

236

terminate Co-Investor's right to possession by notice in writing, and Investor may enforce all of his rights and remedies under this Agreement, including his right to recover rent as it becomes due. Investor's rights hereunder shall be in addition to those provided in the default section of Exhibit A attached hereto.

(b) If Co-Investor fails to make any payment within ten (10) days after notice of default is set forth in Paragraph 6 (a) above or defaults on any of his obligations under Paragraph 6 (b) or (c) above, the entire amount of monthly payments due for the term of the lease under Paragraph 4 (f), plus the entire value of Investor's investment as set forth in Paragraph 3, shall become immediately due and payable to Investor and Investor may foreclose on the Deed of Trust as set forth in Paragraph 4 (c) above.

Upon the sale or repurchase by Investor of Co-Investor's one-half interest in the premises, Co-Investor shall be deemed a month-to-month tenant as to the entire premises and shall be obligated to pay to Investor as rent an amount equal to all principal, interest, insurance, tax and assessment payments due on such property, until his leasehold interest in the premises is terminated as set forth in Paragraph 7 (a) and/or Exhibit A.

(c) Co-Investor acknowledges that if any monthly payment due from Co-Investor is not received by holders of notes when due, Investor shall incur costs the exact amount of which is extremely difficult and impractical to fix. Therefore, Co-Investor shall pay to Investor an additional sum of six (6) percent of the overdue rent and purchase payment as a late charge. The parties agree that this late charge represents a fair and reasonable estimate of the costs that Investor will incur by reason of late payment by Co-Investor. Acceptance of any late charge shall not constitute a waiver of Co-Investor's default with respect to the overdue amount, or prevent Investor from exercising any of the other rights and remedies available to him.

8. DEFAULT BY CO-INVESTOR

Upon the signing of this Agreement, a Request for Notice of Default shall be given to all lenders on behalf of the Investor. If the Co-Investor fails to make said payments within ten (10) days after Notice has been given by the Investor, Investor can cure the default at Co-Investor's cost. Any sums paid by the Investor shall be due immediately from the Co-Investor, and if not paid shall bear interest at the rate of six (6) percent per annum until paid.

If Co-Investor does not cure his default within ten (10) days after Notice has been given by Investor, Investor may thereafter, at his option, make all purchase payments directly to the holder(s) of the Note(s) and policies of insurance covering the premises and to the appropriate governmental authority for tax and assessment payments due on such property.

9. OPTIONS TO PURCHASE OR SELL

Each party shall have the right to purchase the interest of the other party in such premises on the following terms and conditions:

(a) At any time during the first twelve (12) months after purchase of the premises, Co-Investor may purchase Investor's interest in the premises in this Agreement for the sum of approximately Thirty Thousand Dollars ($30,000).

(b) At any time during the thirteenth (13th) through the twenty-fourth (24th) month after purchase of the premises, Co-Investor may purchase Investor's interest in the premises in this Agreement for the sum of Forty Thousand Dollars ($40,000).

(c) At any time during the twenty-fifth (25th) through the thirty-sixth (36th) month after purchase of the premises, Co-Investor may purchase Investor's interest in the premises in this Agreement for the sum of Fifty Thousand Dollars ($50,000).

(d) If Co-Investor should elect not to purchase Investor's one-half interest as set forth in Paragraph 9 (b) or 9 (c), Investor shall have the option to purchase Co-Investor's one-half interest for the same amount as stated in Paragraph 9 (b) or 9 (c), minus the Investor's investment. This option shall expire unless exercised in writing at least sixty (60) days prior to the initial date of termination of this agreement as set forth in Paragraph 1 above.

(e) By mutual agreement Investor and Co-Investor may extend this contract for an additional period of time.

(f) Should Investor and Co-Investor elect none of the above, it is agreed by both parties that the property shall be sold at the appraised value. Upon the sale of the property, the net proceeds shall be distributed as follows:

> Investor's investment plus ½ of first year appreciation.
>
> Investor's investment plus ½ of first two years appreciation (combined).

(1) Investor shall first receive a sum equal to his investment, including costs, as set forth in Paragraph 3, and reimbursement for the Investor's share of the Home Warranty policy, and any other monies expended by the Investor on the property.

(2) The remainder of the sales price shall be divided equally between Investor and Co-Investor after all costs of the sale have been deducted.

238

(g) All options stated in Paragraph 9 (a), (b), (c), (d), (e), and (f) shall be in writing and given to the respective party at least sixty (60) days prior to the expiration of said option.

10. NOTICES

Any and all notices and other communications required or permitted by this Agreement shall be served on or given to either party by the other party in writing and shall be deemed duly served and given when personally delivered to any of the parties to whom it is directed, or in lieu of such personal service, when deposited in the United States mail, first class postage prepaid, addressed to Investor at _____ or Co-Investor at the property address or such forwarding address that the Co-Investor has given to the Investor.

11. ATTORNEY'S FEES

In the event any legal action is brought by either party to enforce the terms hereof or relating to the demised premises, the prevailing party shall be entitled to all costs incurred in connection with such action, including reasonable attorney's fees as determined by the Court.

Dated: _____

_____   _____
INVESTOR   CO-INVESTOR

_____   _____
INVESTOR   CO-INVESTOR

STATE OF CALIFORNIA
COUNTY OF TUOLUMNE

On _____ , before me, the undersigned, a Notary Public in and for said County and State, personally appeared _____ , known to me to be the person(s) whose name(s) is (are) subscribed to the within instrument and acknowledged that _____ executed the same.

_____
Notary Signature Line

LEASE-OPTION/EQUITY-SHARING AGREEMENT

THIS AGREEMENT is made _____ , between _____ and _____ ,

239

husband and wife, hereinafter called LESSEE/BUYER, AND _____ , hereinafter called LESSOR/SELLER.

This agreement modifies and supersedes Residential Lease with Option to Purchase executed by and between the same parties and dated January 26, 1982. Any inconsistent provisions as between this Agreement and aforementioned agreement shall be controlled by this Agreement. Receipt is hereby acknowledged from Lessee/Buyer of $400 option consideration, and six monthly payments of $550 each, said payments to be credited as follows: $1,500 to option consideration and $1,800 to rent.

LEASE OPTION:

1. SUBJECT PROPERTY:

(a) Lessor/Seller hereby leases to Lessee/Buyer that certain real property commonly known as _____ , Modesto, California, and which is more particularly described as: Lot 6 in Block 6918 of MONTGOMERY VILLAGE NO. 1, as per Map thereof filed June 14, 1957, in Volume 18 of Maps, page 69, Stanislaus County Records.

2. TERMS:

(a) The term of this lease shall be for a period of one year, commencing on the first day of March 1982, and ending on the 28th day of February 1983.

3. RENT:

(a) Lessee/Buyer shall pay Lessor/Seller as rent for subject premises the sum of $550 per month, commencing on the 1st day of March 1982 and a like amount to be due on the 1st day of each succeeding month during the term hereof. Payment shall be presented to Lessor/Seller or her agent or assignee at _____ , Modesto, California 95350, or a designated place.

4. POSSESSION:

(a) Possession was delivered to Lessee/Buyer on March 1, 1982.

5. OPTION TO PURCHASE:

(a) Lessor/Seller grants Lessee/Buyer, subject to the provisions of Paragraphs 7 and 8 the right to purchase at any time during the time period of February 1, 1983, through February 28, 1986, an UNDIVIDED ONE-

HALF INTEREST in said property, conditioned upon full compliance by Lessee/Buyer with all terms of this Agreement.

(b) Lessee/Buyer agrees to pay $3,400 to Lessor/Seller in lawful U.S. currency as consideration for Lessor/Seller granting Lessee/Buyer an option to purchase said property. This consideration shall be paid as follows: $400 prior to occupancy, receipt of which was previously acknowledged. (This amount is in addition to the rent as specified in Paragraph 3 above.) Lessor/Seller agrees that upon exercise of the option Lessee/Buyer shall be credited with $250 from each monthly rental payment of $550 (as specified in Paragraph 3 above) toward the option consideration. Should the option not be exercised by Lessee/Buyer, there will be no refund of any option consideration.

(c) The purchase price of the property shall be in an amount equal to $33,475, which is one-half the agreed upon value of $66,950 for subject property.

6. ENCUMBRANCES:

(a) The only encumbrance against said real property is: $9,000 (approximate) 1st loan due to Western Mortgage Co., P.O. Box 54617, Los Angeles, California. Said loan is FHA insured, and has a level interest rate of 5½ percent per annum and is assumable at the Lessee/Buyer's option. The parties agree that neither will cause or permit any lien to attach to or exist on or against the subject property which shall or may be superior to the right of either party or to encumber the property in any manner without having obtained the written consent of the other.

7. EXERCISE OF OPTION:

(a) The option may be exercised by Lessee/Buyer, if at all, as long as Lessee/Buyer is not in default of the terms and conditions of this agreement as enumerated under Paragraph 18. To exercise the option Lessee/Buyer must notify Lessor/Seller in writing of such acceptance. Lessee/Buyer should mail the notification to Lessor/Seller at _____ or a designated place. The postmark must be no later than _____ .

8. TITLE:

(a) Within five (5) days upon receipt of written notification by Lessee/Buyer to exercise the option, Lessor/Seller shall execute and deliver to TRANSAMERICA TITLE COMPANY OF MODESTO all documents required to transfer title to an undivided one-half interest to subject real property along with appropriate escrow instructions. Escrow shall be deemed "open" as of the date of Lessor/Seller's delivery.

(b) Lessee/Buyer's duty to perform hereunder, after exercise of the option, is contingent upon title to the property being insurable as free and clear of all liens, encumbrances or other clouds on title to the property, except:

(1) General and special taxes for the fiscal year in which the escrow closes;

(2) Exceptions, as agreed to by Lessee/Buyer, to be contained in the title report and all current easements, covenants and restrictions of record.

(c) Lessee/Buyer shall have fifteen (15) days from receipt of a title report to examine the title to the property and to report in writing any valid objections thereto. Any exceptions to the title which would be disclosed by examination of the record shall be deemed to have been accepted unless reported in writing within said fifteen (15) days. If Lessee/Buyer objects to any exceptions to the title, Lessor/Seller shall use due diligence to remove such exceptions at her own expense before close of escrow. But if such exceptions cannot be removed before close of escrow, all rights and obligations hereunder may, at the election of Lessee/Buyer, terminate and end, by Lessee/Buyer to rescind the contract because of title exceptions, Lessor/Seller shall refund the option consideration as follows: $400 plus any amounts paid by Lessee/Buyer in excess of the fair and reasonable monthly rental as specified in Paragraph 20 (a), "Holding Over." At the expiration of said 15-day period for examination of title, Lessee/Buyer shall be deemed to have accepted such title in the absence of the required written objections.

9. ESCROW:

(a) Upon both parties' agreement to consummate the sale, appropriate documents shall be recorded and escrow shall close within 45 days from the opening thereof. If escrow is not closed prior to the scheduled closing date or Lessee/Buyer has not complied with the terms of this agreement within forty-five (45) days after escrow is opened, escrow shall be cancelled and this agreement shall be null and void. Lessee/Buyer, Lessor/Seller or escrow holder, as applicable, shall perform the following duties prior to close of escrow:

(1) Lessor/Seller shall deliver to escrow holder an executed grant deed to the property in recordable form conveying an undivided one-half interest in the property to Lessee/Buyer. Parties shall hold title as Tenants in Common.

(2) Escrow holder shall obtain from TRANSAMERICA TITLE COMPANY OF MODESTO a standard form joint protection CLTA policy of title insurance insuring Lessor/Seller's interest in the Deed of Trust and Lessee/Buyer's title in the property in the amount of the purchase price of the property as set forth herein, showing title to an undivided one-half interest in the property vested in Lessee/Buyer subject only to those exceptions to title described in Paragraph 8 (b) above.

(3) Escrow holder shall credit Lessee/Buyer with the OPTION CONSIDERATION accumulated and held by Lessor/Seller during the option period, and said option consideration so credited shall be deducted from the purchase price.

(b) In the event Lessee/Buyer shall have exercised the option in the manner aforementioned herein, and Lessee/Buyer shall not have closed this escrow on the Scheduled Closing Date for a reason other than Lessor/Seller's failure to deliver a Grant Deed to an undivided one-half interest in the property to escrow holder as required by Paragraph 9 (a) (1) above, or the inability of escrow holder to obtain a policy of title insurance to insure title in Lessee/Buyer, subject only to those exceptions to title described in the policy of title or as otherwise described in Paragraph 8 (a) above, then: (1) Lessee/Buyer shall have no right, title, or interest in the property; (2) Lessee/Buyer shall be liable to Lessor/Seller for all damages caused by Lessee/Buyer's wrongful failure to close escrow unless Lessor/Seller shall be in breach; (3) this escrow shall be automatically terminated without further instructions from any party hereto; and (4) escrow holder shall return all items to the party who deposited such items into escrow, without further instruction from either party hereto. Notwithstanding the above, Lessor/Seller may demand that Lessee/Buyer execute cancellation instructions prepared by escrow holder in the event an escrow established pursuant hereto is not closed on or before the Scheduled Closing Date, for a reason other than described in this paragraph.

10. PRORATIONS, CLOSING COSTS, ASSUMPTIONS AND REFINANCING EXPENSES

(a) Real property taxes on the property and general and special

243

assessments, if any, for the current fiscal year shall be prorated to the close of escrow.

(b) The "closing costs" shall be those costs incurred in conjunction with closing escrow and shall be paid at the close of escrow as follows:

(1) All closing costs shall be paid one-half by Lessor/Seller and one-half by Lessee/Buyer except all assumption fees imposed by the secured lien holder set forth in Paragraph 6. If Lessee/Buyer elects to formally assume said loans of record, costs shall be paid fully by Lessee/Buyer.

(2) Any charges, prepayment penalties or expenses imposed by the terms of the underlying Deed of Trust and promissory note of the lien holder set forth in Paragraph 5 in the event Lessee/Buyer elects to refinance or to pay off said encumbrance shall be paid by Lessor/Seller.

(3) In the event escrow does not close on the Scheduled Closing Date or another mutually agreed upon date thereafter, the closing costs incurred through the escrow to such date shall be the responsibility of the party at fault. In the event escrow shall fail to close on the Scheduled Closing Date or another mutually agreed upon closing date due to fault of **both** parties or **neither** party to this agreement, the costs of terminating the escrow shall be divided equally between the parties.

11. ACCELERATION OF PAYMENT:

(a) Said underlying loans are currently assumable at the option of Lessee/Buyer.

12. REPAIRS AND CONDITION OF PROPERTY DURING LEASE PERIOD:

(a) Lessee/Buyer accepts the premises as being in good condition and repair. Lessee/Buyer, at Lessee/Buyer's cost and without obligation to Lessor/Seller shall keep and maintain the premises, and every part thereof, in good and satisfactory repair and condition, reasonable wear and tear excepted, during the term of the lease. Lessee/Buyer shall indemnify and hold Lessor/Seller harmless from any and all mechanics liens or claims of lien and all attorneys fees, costs and expenses which may accrue, grow out of, or be incurred by reason of or on account of such lien or claim of lien.

(b) Subject property is represented by Lessor/Seller to Lessee/Buyer as having no physical defects of which Lessor/Seller is aware, that are of a magnitude that should be disclosed to Lessee/Buyer.

13. INDEMNIFICATION:

(a) Lessor/Seller shall not be liable for any damage or injury to Lessee/Buyer or any other person, or to any property, occurring on the premises, or any part thereof, or in common areas thereof, unless such damage is the approximate result of the negligence or unlawful act of Lessor/Seller, their agents or employees. Lessee/Buyer agrees to hold Lessor/Seller harmless from any claims for damages no matter how caused, except for injury or damages for which Lessor/Seller is legally responsible, so long as Lessee/Buyer remains in possession of the premises.

14. UTILITIES:

(a) Lessee/Buyer shall be responsible for the payment of all utilities and services.

15. LOSS:

(a) Lessor/Seller shall maintain a policy of fire insurance in the amount of $ _____ insuring the premises from loss by fire, flood, earthquake or other disaster during the lease period and to close of escrow. Any loss to the real property or personal property (exclusive of Lessee/Buyer's furnishings and personal belongings) contained therein for any reason whatsoever, including condemnation by any governmental agency, fire, flood, earthquake, or whatever, which is not covered by Lessor/Seller's policy of insurance, will be apportioned between the parties as to their interests pursuant to this agreement.

16. ORDINANCES AND STATUTES:

(a) Lessee/Buyer shall comply with all statutes, ordinances and requirements of all municipal, state and federal authorities now in force, or which may hereafter be in force, pertaining to the use of the premises.

17. LATE CHARGES:

(a) Lessee/Buyer acknowledges that late payment of rent will cause Lessor/Seller to incur costs not contemplated by this lease, the exact amount of which is extremely difficult to ascertain. If any installment of rent is more than TEN (10) days past due, Lessee/Buyer shall pay Lessor/Seller a late charge equal to 5 percent of such past due amount. The parties agree that such late charge represents a fair and reasonable estimate of the costs Lessor/Seller incurred for extra accounting charges and late charges imposed by lenders of record.

18. DEFAULT:

(a) The occurrence of any of the following shall constitute a material default and breach of lease by Lessee/Buyer.

(1) Monthly lease payments must be paid in a timely fashion, i.e. on or before the 1st day of each month. If Lessee/Buyer is more than TEN (10) days late on more than three of the monthly payments and Lessor/Seller has not agreed in writing to extensions on the appropriate due dates, Lessor/Seller will treat the failure to pay in a timely fashion as a breach of condition of the contract and may refuse to convey title, even if there are no payments in default at the time Lessee/Buyer attempts to exercise the option to purchase. If the lease is in substantial default (90% or more of any monthly increment past due) at the time the option period matures, Lessor/Seller may refuse to convey title. CREDITWORTHI-NESS OF LESSEE/BUYER IS OF THE ESSENCE IN THE LEASE-OPTION PORTION OF THIS CONTRACT. CREDITWORTHINESS WILL BE BASED UPON LESSEE/BUYER'S REGULAR AND TIMELY PAYMENTS OF MONTHLY LEASE OBLIGATIONS AS SPECIFIED ABOVE.

(2) Any failure by Lessee/Buyer to perform any other provision of this lease to be performed by Lessee/Buyer where such failure continues THIRTY (30) days after written notice thereof by Lessor/Seller will constitute a material breach of this contract.

19. REMEDIES UPON DEFAULT:

(a) In the event of any such default by Lessee/Buyer, then in addition to any other remedies available to Lessor/Seller at law or in equity, Lessor/Seller shall have the option to terminate this lease and all rights hereunder by giving written notice of intention to terminate.

20. HOLDING OVER:

(a) Any holding over after the expiration of the term of the lease in the event Lessee/Buyer's option to purchase is not exercised or upon the exercise of Lessor/Seller's option to terminate the lease pursuant to the Default provisions of Paragraphs 15 and 16, shall be construed to be

a tenancy from month to month at a monthly rental of $ _____ .
The parties have bargained for and agree that said monthly sum of
$ _____ is a fair and reasonable monthly rental for the negotiated
anticipation of the parties that Lessee/Buyer would exercise the option to
purchase prior to termination.

21. NOTICES:

(a) Any and all notices and other communications required
or permitted by this agreement shall be served on or given to either
party by the other party in writing and shall be deemed duly served and
given when personally delivered to any of the parties to whom it is
directed, or in lieu of such personal service, when deposited in the United
States mail first class postage prepaid, addressed to Lessor/Seller at
_____ or Lessee/Buyer at the prop-
erty address or such forwarding address that Lessee/Buyer has given to
Lessor/Seller.

22. ASSIGNMENT:

(a) Lessee/Buyer shall not assign, sublet, transfer, mortgage,
pledge, hypothecate or encumber this lease, or any interest in it, without
written permission of Lessor/Seller. Written permission prior to assigning,
subletting, transferring, mortgaging, pledging, hypothecating or encumbering this lease is a condition precedent to the validity of same.

23. WAIVER:

(a) The waiver by Lessor/Seller of any provision of this agreement
shall not constitute a waiver of any other provision of this agreement or any
future waiver of the same provision.

24. AGREEMENT TO EQUITY SHARE:

(a) It is agreed that what parties have bargained for is a fixed lease
on property between Lessor/Seller and Lessee/Buyer. Additionally,
Lessee/Buyer will have, upon proper performance under the lease, an
option to purchase an undivided one-half interest in the property. Upon
exercise of the option, Lessor/Seller and Lessee/Buyer will hold title to
property as Tenants in Common under a plan commonly called "Equity
Sharing." All conditions of the lease-option agreement, including, but not
limited to, the exercise of the option in a timely manner, opening of escrow,
and tendering of appropriate monies and documents into escrow are conditions precedent to the existence of an agreement for Equity Sharing. After

conveyance of title shall have been effected, the following provisions of Equity Sharing will take effect.

EQUITY SHARING

25. TERM:

(a) The term of this agreement for Equity Sharing shall be for a period of from close of escrow unless otherwise agreed upon by parties in writing.

26. SALE OF INTEREST:

(a) As previously stated, Lessor/Seller shall convey to Lessee/ Buyer an undivided one-half interest in said property as Tenants in Common.

27. ENCUMBRANCES:

(a) Lessee/Buyer acknowledges their one-half interest in the property is subject to loans in the approximate amount of $ _____ ; Lessee/Buyer's liability will be in proportion to their interest in the property.

(b) Lessee/Buyer agrees to pay to Lessor/Seller for the term of the equity sharing agreement, monthly payments of _____

_____

_____

_____

_____

_____

(c) Lessee/Buyer will execute a note for an amount equal to the purchase price for an undivided one-half interest in the property, minus option consideration, secured by an All-Inclusive Deed of Trust encumbering subject property. The interest rate of said note shall be _____ per annum. Both note and/or Trust Deed shall contain the following provisions:

(1) An alienation clause to read: If the trustor shall sell, convey or alienate said property, or any part thereof, or any interest therein, or shall be divested of his title or any interest therein in any manner or way, whether voluntarily or involuntarily, without the written consent of the beneficiary being first had and obtained, beneficiary shall have the right, at its option, to declare any indebtedness or obligations secured hereby, irrespective of

the maturity date specified in any note evidencing the same, immediately due and payable.

(2) A late payment clause calling for a charge to Lessor/Seller of $5.00 or 6 percent of the payment, whichever is greater when payment is more than 10 days late.

(d) Said monthly payments shall be credited as follows:

(1) The first _____ of the payment shall be deemed to be a purchase payment to Lessor/Seller for Lessee/Buyer's one-half interest in the subject property. The remainder of the payment, _____ , shall be a lease payment to Lessor/Seller for the one-half interest retained by them in the property.

Any partial or late payments shall be applied first to late charges under Paragraph 17, secondly to rent, and any remainder to monthly purchase payments. Lessor/Seller or their assignee shall make all payments to all beneficiaries and for taxes, upon receipt of the monthly payment received from Lessee/Buyer. Such monthly payment shall be automatically adjusted to reflect changes in taxes. Payments shall be due on the first day of every month and shall be delinquent if not received by Lessor/Seller or her designee by the fifth day of each month.

(2) Lessee/Buyer agrees to execute said note and Deed of Trust in favor of Lessor/Seller for the purpose of securing:

(i) Payment to Lessor/Seller of the indebtedness set forth in Paragraph 27 (c) above.

(ii) The performance of each agreement of Lessee/Buyer incorporated by reference or contained herein. Deed of Trust is to name TRANSAMERICA TITLE COMPANY OF MODESTO as Trustee.

(e) Lessee/Buyer agrees to maintain said property at their sole expense and not make any improvements without the written consent of Lessor/Seller. Major capital improvements as defined in Paragraph 36 must conform to that paragraph.

(f) Lessee/Buyer shall not dispose of any real property or personal property attached thereto connected with the home without written consent of Lessor/Seller.

(g) Lessee/Buyer agrees to sign a lease agreement for Lessor/Seller's one-half interest for _____ or until the property is sold, unless terminated earlier with the consent of Lessor/Seller or by the purchase by Lessee/Buyer of Lessor/Seller's interest in the property. Said lease is attached hereto as Addendum "A" and is fully incorporated herein.

(h) At the signing of this agreement, Lessee/Buyer shall pay for a one-year Homeowners Insurance Policy naming Lessor/Seller as co-insured. Fire insurance coverage shall not be less than $ _____ . Said coverage shall be renewed annually by Lessee/Buyer.

(i) In the event of a total loss, Lessee/Buyer shall assign his interest or any monies paid by the insurance company to Lessor/Seller to cover their investment. Any excess monies will be divided equally between Lessor/Seller and Lessee/Buyer.

(j) In the event of a loss of any personal property, Lessor/Seller agrees to assign their interest of any monies paid by the insurance company to Lessee/Buyer.

28. ENCUMBRANCES AND ASSIGNMENTS:

(a) Lessee/Buyer shall not sell, transfer, assign or encumber his interest in the property, this agreement, or his lease of the property without the prior written consent of Lessor/Seller.

29. DEFAULT BY LESSEE/BUYER:

(a) The occurrence of any of the following shall constitute a default by Lessee/Buyer:

(1) Failure to make any payment under Paragraph 27 (b) or 27 (c) when due, if the failure continues for five (5) days after notice has been given to Lessee/Buyer.

(2) Abandonment and vacation of the premises (failure to occupy the premises for thirty (30) consecutive days) shall be deemed abandonment and vacation, unless notice to Lessor/Seller is given in advance.

(3) Failure to perform any other provision of this Agreement and Addendum "A" if the failure to perform is not cured within five (5) days after notice has been given by Lessor/Seller.

(b) Notices given under this paragraph shall specify the alleged default and the applicable agreement provisions, and shall demand that Lessee/Buyer perform the provisions of this Agreement or make the lease or purchase payment that is in arrears, as the case may be, within the applicable period of time, or quit the premises. No such notice shall be deemed a forfeiture or a termination of this Agreement unless Lessor/Seller so elects in the notice.

30. LESSOR/SELLER'S REMEDIES IN CASE OF DEFAULT:

(a) Lessor/Seller shall have the following remedies if Lessee/Buyer commits default. These remedies are not exclusive; they are cumulative in addition to any remedies now or later allowed by law.

(1) If Lessee/Buyer commits ANY DEFAULT under Paragraph 29 herein, Lessor/Seller may terminate the lease provisions of this Agreement and regain possession of the premises in the manner provided by the laws of unlawful detainer in the State of California in effect at the date of such default. Lessee/Buyer and Lessor/Seller agree that the unlawful detainer action may be instituted for failure to pay rent under the lease agreement OR for failure to pay on the obligation to Lessee/Buyer enumerated in Paragraph 27 (c). As noted in the lease between Lessor/Seller and Lessee/Buyer regarding the Equity Sharing Agreement, payment of the indebtedness to Lessor/Seller (per Paragraph 27 (c)) is a covenant of the lease, failure of which will constitute a material breach of contract in support of an unlawful detainer action. Lessee/Buyer agrees that his right to possession of the premises shall terminate by such default, notwithstanding their ownership interest in one-half of the premises. At Lessor/Seller's option, they may continue the lease provisions of this Agreement in effect for so long as Lessor/Seller does not terminate Lessee/Buyer's right to possession by notice in writing, and Lessor/Seller may enforce all of her rights and remedies under this Agreement, including her right to recover the rent as it becomes due. Lessor/Seller's rights hereunder shall be in addition to those provided in the default section of Addendum "A" attached hereto.

(2) If Lessee/Buyer fails to make payment within five (5) days after notice of default as set forth in Paragraph 29 (a) (1) or defaults on any of their obligations under Paragraph 29 (a) (2) above, the entire amount of monthly payments due for the term of the lease under Paragraph 27 (f), plus the entire balance owing Lessor/Seller under the obligation specified in Paragraph 27 (c) shall become immediately due and payable to Lessor/Seller and Lessor/Seller may foreclose on the note and Deed of Trust as set forth in Paragraph 27 (c) above. Upon the sale or repurchase by Lessor/Seller of Lessee/Buyer's one-half interest in the premises, if Lessee/Buyer

is still in possession of the premises, Lessee/Buyer shall be deemed a month-to-month tenant as to the entire premises and shall be obligated to pay to Lessor/Seller as rent an amount equal to $ _____ as stated in Paragraph 20 (a).

(3) Lessee/Buyer acknowledges that if any monthly payment due from Lessee/Buyer is not received within ten (10) days from date due, Lessor/Seller will incur costs the exact amount of which is extremely difficult and impractical to fix. Therefore, Lessee/Buyer shall pay to Lessor/Seller an additional sum of 10 percent (10%) of the overdue rent and purchase payment as a late charge to accrue on the portion due Lessor/Seller. The parties agree that this late charge represents a fair and reasonable estimate of the costs that Lessor/Seller will incur by reason of late payment by Lessee/Buyer. Acceptance of any late charge shall not constitute a waiver of Lessee/Buyer's default with respect to the overdue amount or prevent Lessor/Seller from exercising any of the other rights and remedies available to her.

31. DEFAULT BY LESSOR/SELLER:

(a) Upon the execution of this Agreement, a request for Notice of Default shall be given to all lenders on behalf of Lessee/Buyer. If Lessor/Seller fails to make any payments on the property when due, he or she shall be in default. If Lessor/Seller fails to make said payments within five (5) days after Notice has been given by Lessee/Buyer, Lessee/Buyer may cure the default at Lessor/Seller's cost. Any sums paid by Lessee/Buyer shall be due immediately from Lessor/Seller and if not paid shall bear interest at the rate of ten percent (10%) per annum until paid.

(b) If Lessor/Seller does not cure their default within five (5) days after Notice has been given by Lessee/Buyer, Lessee/Buyer may thereafter, at their option, make all purchase payments directly to the holder(s) of the Note(s) and policies of insurance covering the premises and to the appropriate governmental authority for tax and assessment payments due on such property.

32. OPTIONS TO PURCHASE OR SELL:

(a) Each party shall have the first right to purchase the interest of the other party in such premises on the following terms and conditions:

(1) After FIVE (5) YEARS from purchase of the premises, Lessee/Buyer may purchase Lessor/Seller's interest in the premises. Upon written notification of intent to purchase by Lessee/Buyer, parties will

ascertain the fair market value of the premises by obtaining an appraisal as provided for in Paragraph 35.

(2) If Lessee/Buyer should elect not to purchase Lessor/Seller's one-half interest, Lessor/Seller shall have the option to purchase Lessee/Buyer's one-half interest for the same price, minus Lessor/Seller's equity.

(3) Should Lessor/Seller and Lessee/Buyer elect none of the above, it is agreed by both parties that the property shall be listed for sale with a licensed Real Estate Broker mutually agreed upon by Lessor/Seller and Lessee/Buyer, at the appraised value. The amount of commission and the term of the listing shall be determined at the time the listing is taken.

(4) Upon either Lessor/Seller's purchasing Lessee/Buyer's interest or Lessee/Buyer purchasing Lessor/Seller's interest, costs will be paid in the same manner as specified in Paragraph 10.

(b) Upon sale of the property to a third party, the price received shall be distributed as follows:

(1) Costs of sale to be deducted, real estate commission (if any), title insurance, escrow, recording fees and transfer tax;

(2) Underlying 1st loan to be paid (including any costs to pay off said loan, e.g. prepayment penalty) unless Buyer assumes the loan;

(3) Any indebtedness by Lessee/Buyer to Lessor/Seller arising from the aforementioned All-Inclusive Trust Deed per Paragraph 27 (c) to be paid;

(4) Remaining funds, if any, to be divided equally between Lessor/Seller and Lessee/Buyer.

(c) By mutual agreement Lessor/Seller and Lessee/Buyer may extend this contract for an additional period of time. Such extension must be in writing and signed by both parties.

(d) All options stated in Paragraph 32 shall be in writing and given to the respective party at least sixty (60) days prior to the expiration of said option.

33. NOTICES:

(a) Any and all notices and other communications required or permitted by this Agreement shall be served on or given to either party by the other party in writing and shall be deemed duly served and given when personally delivered to any of the parties to whom it is directed, or in lieu of such personal service, when deposited in the United States Mail, first class postage prepaid, addressed to Lessor/Seller at _____ or Lessee/Buyer at the property address or such forwarding address that Lessee/Buyer has given to Lessor/Seller.

34. ARBITRATION:

(a) Any controversy between the parties to this Agreement, involving the construction or application of any of the terms, provisions, or conditions of this Agreement, shall on the written request of either party served on the other be submitted to arbitration and such arbitration shall comply with and be governed by the provisions of the California Arbitration Act, Sections 1280–1294.2 of the California Code of Civil Procedure. The parties shall each appoint one person to hear and determine the dispute and, if they are unable to agree, the two persons so chosen shall select a third impartial arbitrator whose decision shall be final and conclusive upon both parties. The cost of arbitration shall be borne by the losing party or in such proportions as the arbitrator shall decide.

35. APPRAISAL:

(a) When necessary, the fair market value shall be determined as the average of two appraisals of the property as described in this paragraph. If possible, the appraisals shall be based on the sale prices of comparable properties in the market area sold within the preceding three-month period. The appraisals shall be made upon request of either party by two independent residential appraisers, one to be selected by Lessor/Seller and one by Lessee/Buyer. Each appraiser shall be approved by the Federal National Mortgage Association. The cost of the appraiser selected by Lessor/Seller shall be borne by Lessor/Seller, and the cost of the appraiser selected by Lessee/Buyer shall be borne by Lessee/Buyer. The fair market value of the property shall be determined as the average of the two appraisals. If Lessee/Buyer fails to select a qualified appraiser within 15 days after Lessor/Seller has notified Lessee/Buyer in writing of Lessor/Seller's request for an appraisal of the property, the reasons therefore, and Lessee/Buyer's option to select an independent appraiser within 15 days after Lessor/Seller's request is submitted to Lessee/Buyer, Lessor/Seller may designate the second appraiser, provided Lessor/Seller's request informs Lessee/Buyer of this time limitation, and that Lessor/Seller will select an appraiser on behalf of Lessee/Buyer in the event Lessee/Buyer fails to designate an appraiser, with consequent cost to Lessee/Buyer. If pursuant to this section Lessor/Seller designates the second appraiser, the cost of both appraisals shall be borne equally by Lessor/Seller and Lessee/Buyer. If in any case the property has been damaged (other than normal wear and tear) and the damage has not been fully repaired, the determination of fair market value shall be based on the condition of the property not including the damage. Nothing in this paragraph shall preclude Lessor/Seller and Lessee/Buyer from establishing fair market value of the property by mutual agreement in lieu of appraisals pursuant to this section.

36. IMPROVEMENTS MADE BY LESSEE/BUYER:

(a) The cost of capital improvements to the property completed within any 12-month period, and with an appraised value in excess of two thousand five hundred dollars ($2,500) shall be added to Lessee/Buyer's share of any final financial gain but only if the procedures set forth in this paragraph are followed.

(b) Within 60 days following the completion of the improvements, Lessee/Buyer shall send by first class mail a notice of the completion of the improvement to the lender, if any, and shall submit proof of cost of the improvements.

(c) Within 90 days following the completion of the improvements, Lessor/Seller shall select an appraiser to perform an appraisal to determine the increase in value of the property, if any, by reason of the improvements. A copy of the appraisal shall be sent by first class mail to Lessee/Buyer, together with a notice informing Lessee/Buyer that the appraisal will constitute a final and conclusive determination of the increase in the value of the property by reason of the improvement for purposes of computing the net appreciated value of the property, and that if Lessee/Buyer disputes the amount of the appraisal, Lessee/Buyer may procure an independent appraisal as provided in Paragraph 35. Lessor/Seller may require Lessee/Buyer to pay for the cost of the appraisal.

(d) If Lessee/Buyer disputes the amount of the appraisal, Lessee/Buyer within 120 days of the completion of the improvements, may secure at Lessee/Buyer's expense, a qualified, independent appraiser to perform an appraisal to determine the increase in value of the property, if any, by reason of the improvements, and a copy of the appraisal shall be sent by first class mail to Lessor/Seller within the period of time.

(e) If the appraisal of the appraiser selected by Lessee/Buyer is greater in amount than the appraisal of the appraiser selected by Lessor/Seller, the amount of the appraisal, for the purposes of this section, shall be one-half of the sum of the two appraisals.

(f) The lesser of Lessee/Buyer's actual cost or the appraised increase in the value of the property by reason of the improvements shall be available as a credit to Lessee/Buyer for purposes of determining net appreciated value.

(g) If 50 percent or more of the value of the labor or other work on the improvements was performed by Lessee/Buyer, then the appraised increase in the value of the property by reason of the improvements shall be the cost of capital improvements for purposes of establishing the credit under this section.

37. FINANCING COSTS:

(a) Lessor/Seller may refinance the property at any time during the six years of this Agreement as long as it does not materially affect this Agreement. If Lessor/Seller chooses to do this prior to Lessee/Buyer exercising this option, Lessor/Seller shall pay all costs of said new financing.

(b) Any financing costs incurred by a party exercising an option shall be borne by that party.

38. TAX CONSIDERATIONS:

(a) It is the parties' intent that the following tax consequences shall result from this Agreement:

(1) Lessor/Seller will recognize ordinary income to the extent the lease payments provided in both Lease Agreements; Lessor/Seller shall be entitled to deductions for all expenses associated with the rental of Lessor/Seller's undivided one-half interest in the property, including but not limited to interest, depreciation, _____ and other expenditures associated with the rental thereof. Lessor/Seller shall recognize ordinary income to the extent of any interest payments received from Lessee/Buyer pursuant to the note referenced in Paragraph 27 (c).

(2) Lessee/Buyer shall be entitled to deductions for payments made to Lessor/Seller for interest relating to their undivided one-half interest in the property and for _____ .

39. SUCCESSORS AND ASSIGNS: ASSIGNMENT:

(a) All terms of this Agreement shall be binding upon the respective successors, heirs or permitted assigns of the parties hereto and shall inure to the benefit of and be enforceable by the parties hereto and their respective successors, heirs, and permitted assigns: provided, that except as otherwise provided in this Agreement, neither this Agreement nor any rights hereunder may be assigned by Lessee/Buyer without the express written consent of Lessor/Seller.

40. ATTORNEYS' FEES:

(a) In the event any legal action is brought by either party to enforce the terms hereof or relating to the demised premises, the prevailing party shall be entitled to all costs incurred in connection with such action, including reasonable attorneys' fees as determined by the Court.

41. LICENSE DISCLOSURE:

(a) Lessor/Sellers are licensed California Real Estate persons acting as principals for their own account.

42. TIME:

(a) Time is of the essence in this lease and the options given hereunder.

43. CHANGE IN EXISTING LEGAL RIGHTS AND OBLIGATIONS:

(a) It is fully understood by the parties hereto that execution of this Agreement can, and likely will, create or change existing legal rights or obligations relative to such things as, but not necessarily limited to, depreciation allowances, property taxes and interest deductions. Therefore, each party hereto should seek the advice of legal counsel before execution of these documents.

44. GENDER, TENSE AND PLURALITY OF WORDS:

(a) All words used in this Agreement, including the words Lessor/Seller and Lessee/Buyer shall be construed to include the plural as well as the singular number; words used herein in the present tense shall include the future as well as the present; and words used in the masculine gender shall include the feminine and neuter.

45. MODIFICATION:

(a) Any modification of any portion of this Agreement must be made in writing and signed by both parties.

46. RECORDING:

(a) If Lessee/Buyer chooses to record a memorandum of this Agreement or the Agreement in its entirety, Lessee/Buyer shall bear such costs. Lessee/Buyer shall also, prior to said recording, execute such documents as required by TRANSAMERICA TITLE COMPANY OF MODESTO that are necessary to clear title to the property should Lessee/Buyer terminate for any reason prior to exercise of the option.

DATED: _____   _____

_____

_____

_____

ADDENDUM "A"

LEASE AGREEMENT

This lease is made _____ by and between _____ , as lessor (hereinafter referred to as "Lessor/Seller") and _____ , as lessee (hereinafter referred to as "Lessee/Buyer"). Lessor/Seller and Lessee/Buyer are to be owners of the premises to be leased. This agreement pertains to the lease of Lessor/Seller's right to possession of the premises to Lessee/Buyer.

1. PREMISES:

(a) The common description is _____ in the County of Stanislaus, _____ .

(b) Lessee/Buyer has inspected the leased premises and accepts same for occupancy in its "AS IS" condition. Neither Lessor/Seller nor any agent or representative of Lessor/Seller has made any warranty or other representation with respect to the lease premises and Lessor/Seller knows of no defects of a magnitude that should be disclosed to Lessee/Buyer.

2. TERM:

(a) The term of this lease shall commence on _____ and ends on _____ , unless terminated earlier in accordance with the provisions of this lease. If Lessor/Seller, for any reason, cannot deliver possession of the leased premises to Lessee/Buyer at the commencement of the term of this lease, this lease shall be void, and Lessor/Seller shall not be liable to Lessee/Buyer for any loss or damage resulting from such failure.

3. RENT:

(a) Lessee/Buyer agrees to pay rent of $ _____ per month in advance on the first day of each month for the leased premises at the address of Lessor/Seller set forth in this lease for the term of this lease.

4. FIRST MONTH'S RENT:

(a) Upon execution of this lease Lessee/Buyer shall pay to Lessor/ Seller the sum of $ _____ .

5. PERMITTED USES:

(a) Lessee/Buyer shall use the leased premises as a single family residence and for no other purposes.

6. PROHIBITED USES:

(a) Lessee/Buyer shall not do or permit anything to be done in or about the leased premises that in any way increases the existing rate of or affects any fire or other insurance on the leased premises or any of its contents, or that causes a cancellation of any insurance policy covering the leased premises or any part of them or any of its contents. Lessee/Buyer shall not commit or cause to be committed any nuisance or waste in or on the leased premises. Lessee/Buyer shall not use the leased premises in any way that will conflict with any law, statute, ordinance or government rule or regulation now in force or which may later be enacted or promulgated.

7. ALTERATIONS:

(a) Lessee/Buyer shall not make or cause to be made any alterations, additions or improvements to any part of the leased premises without the prior written consent of Lessor/Seller.

8. LIENS:

(a) Lessee/Buyer shall keep the leased premises and the property on which the leased premises are situated free from any liens arising out of any work performed, materials furnished or obligations incurred by Lessee/Buyer.

9. ASSIGNMENT AND SUBLETTING:

(a) Lessee/Buyer shall not assign, transfer, mortgage, pledge, hypothecate or encumber this lease, or any interest in it. Lessee/Buyer shall not sublet the leased premises or any part of them, or cause any other person to occupy or use the leased premises or any part of them, without the written consent of Lessor/Seller. A consent to one assignment or subletting shall not be deemed to be a consent to any later assignment or subletting. Any assignment or subletting without the consent shall be void, and, at the option of Lessor/Seller, shall terminate this lease. This lease and any interest in it shall not be assignable as to the interest of Lessee/Buyer by operation of law, without the written consent of Lessor/Seller.

10. WAIVER OF CLAIMS:

(a) Lessor/Seller shall not be liable to Lessee/Buyer and Lessee/Buyer waives all claims against Lessor/Seller for any injury or damage to any person or property in or about the leased premises by or from any cause.

11. HOLD HARMLESS:

(a) Lessee/Buyer shall hold Lessor/Seller harmless from and defend Lessee/Buyer against any and all claims or liability for any injury or damage to any person or property when such injury or damage shall be caused, or alleged to be caused, in part or in whole by the act, neglect or fault of Lessee/Buyer, their agents, servants, employees or invitees.

12. INSURANCE:

(a) _____ shall maintain public liability and property damage insurance protecting them from liability in an amount not less than Three Hundred Thousand Dollars ($300,000). In addition, _____ shall maintain insurance protecting Lessor/Seller from loss for the destruction of the improvements on the leased premises in an amount not less than $ _____ . Cost of said insurance is to be $ _____ .

260

13. UTILITIES:

(a) Lessee/Buyer shall pay for all water, gas, heat, light, power, telephone service and all other services and utilities supplied to the leased premises.

14. MAINTENANCE:

(a) Lessee/Buyer, at their sole cost, shall maintain the leased premises and every part of them in good and sanitary condition and repair, and shall repair all damage resulting from use by Lessee/Buyer or any person caused to be on the leased premises by Lessee/Buyer.

15. TAXES:

(a) Lessor/Seller shall pay, before delinquency, all property taxes assessed for or during the term of this lease. Lessee/Buyer shall reimburse Lessor/Seller for the cost of said taxes in accordance with the provisions of Paragraph 27 (b) of the attached agreement, "Lease-Option/Equity-Sharing Agreement."

16. HOLDING OVER:

(a) If, with Lessor/Seller's consent, Lessee/Buyer holds possession of the leased premises after the term of this lease, Lessee/Buyer shall become a tenant from month to month on the terms specified in this lease and Paragraph 20 (a) of attached agreement.

17. ENTRY BY LESSOR/SELLER:

(a) Lessor/Seller reserves and shall at any and all times have the right to enter the leased premises to inspect them. Lessor/Seller shall give Lessee/Buyer reasonable notice before making any such entry. Lessee/Buyer waives any claim for damages for any loss of occupancy or quiet enjoyment of the leased premises.

18. DEFAULT BY LESSEE/BUYER:

(a) The occurrence of any of the following shall constitute a material default and breach of this lease by Lessee/Buyer:

(1) Any failure by Lessee/Buyer to pay the rent or to make any other payment required to be made by Lessee/Buyer under this lease, including payment of the obligated to Lessor/Seller under Paragraph 27 (b) and (c) of Lease-Option/Equity-Sharing Agreement attached.

261

(2) The abandonment or vacation of the leased premises by Lessee/Buyer.

(3) A failure by Lessee/Buyer to observe and perform any other provisions of this lease that is to be observed or performed by Lessee/Buyer.

(b) In case of any such default by Lessee/Buyer, then in addition to any other remedies available to Lessor/Seller at law or in equity, Lessor/Seller shall have the immediate option to terminate this lease and all rights of Lessee/Buyer under it by giving written notice of the intention to terminate in the manner specified in Paragraph 21 of this lease. If Lessor/Seller elects to terminate this lease, then Lessor/Seller may recover from Lessee/Buyer.

(1) The worth at the time of award of any unpaid rent which had been earned after termination until the time of such termination; plus

(2) The worth at the time of award of the amount by which the unpaid rent which would have been earned after termination until the time of award exceeds the amount of such rental loss Lessee/Buyer proves could have been reasonably avoided; plus

(3) The worth at the time of award of the amount by which the unpaid rent for the balance of the term after the time of award exceeds the amount of such rental loss that Lessee/Buyer proves could reasonably be avoided; plus

(4) Any other amount necessary to compensate Lessor/Seller for all the detriment proximity caused by Lessor/Seller's failure to perform their obligations under this lease or which in the ordinary course of things would be likely to result from such failure; plus

(5) Such other amounts in addition to or in lieu of any of the above items as may be permitted from time to time by applicable California law. As used in subparagraphs (1) and (2) above, the "worth at the time of award" is computed by allowing interest at the rate of ten percent (10%) per annum. As used in subparagraph (3) above, the "worth at the time of award" is computed by discounting such amount at the discount rate of the Federal Reserve Bank of San Francisco at the time of the award plus one percent (1%).

(c) In case of any such default by Lessee/Buyer, Lessor/Seller shall also have the right, with or without terminating this lease, to reenter the

262

premises and remove all persons and property from the premises; such property may be removed and stored in a public warehouse or elsewhere at the cost of and for the account of Lessee/Buyer.

19. ATTORNEYS' FEES:

(a) In case of any action or proceeding brought by either party against the other under this lease, the prevailing party shall be entitled to recover for the fees of its attorneys in such action or proceeding such amount as the court may adjudge reasonable attorneys' fees.

20. WAIVER:

(a) The waiver by Lessor/Seller of the breach of Lessee/Buyer of any term, covenants, or condition in this lease shall not be deemed to be a waiver of any later breach of the same or any other term, covenant or condition.

21. NOTICES:

(a) All communications, notices and demands of any kind that either party may be required or desires to give to or serve on the other party shall be made in writing and sent by registered mail to the following addresses:

LESSOR/SELLER:

LESSEE/BUYER:

Any such notice shall be presumed to have been received by the addressee 48 hours after posting in the United States mail. Either party may change its address by giving the other party written notice of its new address.

22. SUCCESSORS AND ASSIGNS:

(a) The covenants and conditions of this lease shall apply to and bind the heirs, successors, executors, administrators and assigns of all the parties to the lease.

23. MISCELLANEOUS:

(a) This lease is governed by the laws of California, and any question arising under it shall be construed or determined according to such law. Headings at the beginning of each numbered paragraph of this lease are solely for the convenience of the parties and are not a part of this lease.

Lessor/Seller and Lessee/Buyer have executed this lease the day and year first written above.

DATED: _____   _____

_____

_____

_____

ACKNOWLEDGMENTS

People who help you realize your dreams are one of life's most valuable assets. With that in mind, I would like to express my appreciation to all those who have given me encouragement, advice, and support along the way. In particular I want to thank my wife, Yolanda, whose hard work and loyalty made all the difference; our children, who inspired us to do more for their sakes; and my parents, who taught me to believe in myself.

In addition, I am especially grateful to those who aided in the preparation of this book: Walter L. Kleine for enthusiasm and patience in research; Vickie Kelley, a super secretary who can read my handwriting; Judy Moretz, whose assistance in organizing material made my job easier; and Fred Hills, my editor at Simon and Schuster, whose suggestions and guidance encouraged all of us.

Index

266

inspectors, for real estate, 98
interest rates, 90, 110, 111, 130
Internal Revenue Service (IRS),
    59
  levied property sales of, 115–18
  liens of, 115–18, 122, 136–39
investment brokers, 84
Investment Comparison Chart, 89
Invitation to Bid forms, 78

jobs, highly paid, 15–18
Jobs Rated Almanac, The
    (Krantz), 17
junior lien holders, 136, 138

knowledge, financial power and,
    29–31, 32
Krantz, Les, 17

Labor Department, U.S., 17
lease options, 163–72, 185
  agreement forms for, 223–33,
    239–63
  agreements for, 164–66, 170–
    171
  with equity sharing, 170–72
  equity-sharing agreement and,
    169, 171, 172
  explanation of, 164–66
  moneymaker, 166
  options and, 163–64
  sandwich, 166–67
  selling on, 169–70
legal notices, 37, 52, 59, 60, 63,
    66, 116, 145
lenders, 105–6, 107, 128–29,
    131–39, 143, 144, 154
Lennon, John, 61
leverage, 88, 90, 91
liens, 115–18, 121–24, 136–39
liquidity, 88, 90, 91
liquor, restrictions on, 51–52
lis pendens, 118–19
loan brokers, 176
loans:
  home equity, 41, 153
  notes as, 173–75, 176
  for personal property, 151–52
  for real estate, 103–14
  see also Federal Housing Ad-

ministration; Veterans Admin-
    istration
lots, 35, 39, 45, 49, 62

McDonald's, 26
mailing lists:
  for auctions, 50–51, 52–53, 56,
    58, 59, 60, 66, 70
  for real estate, 108–9, 116, 119,
    120, 140
market value, buying below, 33–
    43
marshal's sales, 59–60
mechanic's liens, 136, 138
media, business, 84
merchandise:
  auction vs. retail, quality of, 37
  disposing of, 45–52, 66
  duty-free, 185
Monaghan, Tom, 20
money:
  making money with, 83–85
  other people's, creative uses of,
    163–72
  saving of, 18–19, 33, 34, 45,
    88–90
  as working for you, 15, 18, 34
Money, 11
mortgage default process, 133–35
mortgages, 103, 127, 131, 154
  insurance for, 103
  payments, 100
  see also Federal Housing Ad-
    ministration; Veterans Admin-
    istration
mortgage states, 131, 133–34,
    135
motivation, 24, 31
motor vehicles, 55, 56, 76
Mrs. Fields cookies, 21

National Asset Seized Forfeiture
    Program, 60
negative cash flow, 19
networking, for partners, 155–59
newspaper notices:
  for auctions, 36–37, 52, 56, 59,
    60, 74, 77
  for foreclosures, 137, 141, 144,
    145, 147–48

About the Author

Dave Del Dotto started out with only two assets: his motivation and a dream. He found that there was no secret to success, just commitment and know-how, and swore that after achieving his financial dreams (it took him only four years), he would share his knowledge with everyone. This successful author, lecturer, and entrepreneur has kept his word. Featured in *Time, Newsweek,* and *Money* magazines, he has been a guest on many national radio and TV shows, and has his own television show (aired from his $5 million dream home in Kona, Hawaii), the longest running financial advisory program in the country.